Start and run a successful

CLEANING
BUSINESS

Start and run a successful

CLEANING BUSINESS

THE ESSENTIAL GUIDE TO BUILDING
A PROFITABLE COMPANY

Robert Gordon

howtobooks

Published by How To Books Ltd
Spring Hill House, Spring Hill Road,
Begbroke, Oxford OX5 1RX, United Kingdom
Tel: (01865) 375794 Fax: (01865) 379162
info@howtobooks.co.uk
www.howtobooks.co.uk

How To Books greatly reduce the carbon footprint of their books by sourcing their typesetting and printing in the UK.

British Library Cataloguing in Publication Data.
A catalogue record for this book is available from the British Library.

ISBN 978 1 84528 284 4

Cover design by Baseline Arts Ltd, Oxford
Produced for How To Books by Deer Park Productions, Tavistock
Typeset by PDQ Typesetting, Newcastle-under-Lyme, Staffordshire
Printed and bound in Great Britain by Bell & Bain Ltd, Glasgow

NOTE: The material contained in this book is set out in good faith for general guidance and no liability can be accepted for loss or expense incurred as a result of relying in particular circumstances on statements made in the book. Laws and regulations are complex and liable to change, and readers should check the current position with the relevant authorities before making personal arrangements.

I would like to thank Joeann, Jim and Gillian
for their help and support in the successes achieved.

CONTENTS

List of illustrations   *xi*
Preface   *xiii*

Chapter 1   **Working in the cleaning industry**   **1**
     Industry facts   1
     Recruiting and retaining staff   2
     Basic skills   2
     Filling the skills gaps in the cleaning sector   3
     Qualifications   3
     Dealing with the franchise problem   5
     Thinking positively   8

Chapter 2   **Deciding between the various cleaning services**   **10**
     Cleaning offices   10
     Cleaning pubs and leisure premises   11
     Builders' cleans   13
     Cleaning new-build homes   14
     Cleaning new-build commercial premises   14
     Domestic cleans   15
     Window cleaning   21
     Cleaning carpets and upholstery   23
     IT (information technology) and specialist cleans   24
     Supplying cleaning consumables   28

Chapter 3   **Starting up**   **31**
     Becoming self-employed   31
     Naming your business   33
     Choosing your legal entity   34
     Working out the initial costs   36
     Deciding where to base yourself   37
     Forget profit: chase success   39
     Creating your brand   40
     Using the telephone   43
     Telephone etiquette   44
     Providing staff uniforms   45

Chapter 4	**Keeping your clients happy**	**46**
	Ensuring client satisfaction	46
	How clients regard cleaning	48
	Anticipating typical complaints	49
	Recognizing problems before they occur	53
	Keeping your clients informed	55
Chapter 5	**Managing your staff**	**57**
	Employing staff	57
	Motivating and rewarding staff	57
	Finding staff	58
	Conducting interviews	61
	Choosing the right place for an interview	63
	Training	64
	Dealing with staff turnover	66
	Your responsibilities as an employer	67
	Your staff's responsibilities	69
Chapter 6	**Organizing your first cleaning account**	**70**
	Visiting your potential client	70
	Making and submitting your quote	72
	Arranging the start date and next meeting	74
	Setting the cleaning schedules	74
	Preparing welcome packs	75
	Organizing your staff	77
	Preparing your cleaning materials	78
	Starting the first shift	79
	Following up	80
Chapter 7	**Ensuring quality of service**	**81**
	Providing your clients with a service	82
	Auditing	83
	Producing detail lists	84
	The importance of following up	86
	Having the right attitude	86
	Conduct and ethics	88
	Application	89
	Dealing with staff problems	90
	No shows	91
	Be proactive and reactive	92

Chapter 8	**Health and safety, laws and regulations**	**95**
	Planning for health and safety	95
	Accidents to cleaners	96
	Complying with employment law	98
	Transfer of Undertakings (Protection of Employment) Regulations 2006 (TUPE)	102
	Applying the national minimum wage	105
	Control of Substances Hazardous to Health Regulations 2002 (COSHH) and colour coding	106
	Reporting of Injuries, Diseases and Dangerous Occurrences Regulations 1995 (RIDDOR)	108
Chapter 9	**Sales, marketing and advertising**	**110**
	Marketing and advertising	110
	Emailing	113
	Organizing stationery and promotional material	115
	Advertising on the Internet	116
	Networking	118
	Making the most of opportunities	119
	Don't stop pushing sales	120
Chapter 10	**Managing finances**	**121**
	Creating business plans	121
	Raising capital	122
	Choosing a bank	123
	Managing your overheads	125
	Buying machinery	125
	Organizing materials and supplies	129
	Bookkeeping	130
	Choosing an accountant	132
	Arranging insurance	133
	Cushions and cautions	135
Chapter 11	**Tax and national insurance**	**136**
	Registering for Value Added Tax (VAT)	136
	National insurance	137
	Deducting tax and managing the payroll	137
	Corporation tax	138
	Income tax	139
	Claiming capital allowances	139
	Working out your business expenses	140

Chapter 12	**Controlling debt**	**141**
	Managing credit	141
	Establishing your invoice dates	142
	Issuing statements	143
	Pursuing debt	143
	Winding-up and bankruptcy petitions	144
	Factoring	145
Chapter 13	**Managing your expansion**	**146**
	Coping with the problems of growth	146
	Recruiting service managers	146
	Employing administrative staff	149
	Managing the payroll	150
	Retaining your clients	152
Chapter 14	**Property services**	**154**
	A lucrative add-on	154
	Offering additional services	155
	Employing a general maintenance operative	159
	Quoted works	160
	Expanding your property services	162
Chapter 15	**Engaging subcontractors**	**164**
	Pros and cons of subcontractors	164
	Finding and choosing subcontractors	165
	Arrangements and agreements	166
	Complying with health and safety requirements	167
	Protecting your clients	168
Appendix I	**Useful contacts**	**169**
Appendix II	**The Cleaning Operators' Proficiency Certificate**	**171**
Appendix III	**Equal opportunities policy**	**173**
Index		*175*

LIST OF ILLUSTRATIONS

1. Pricing matrix   17
2. IT equipment cleaning price list   25
3. Logos   40
4. Cleaning staff database   59
5. Advertising card   61
6. Cleaning quote   73
7. Cleaning schedule   76
8. The audit process   84
9. Audit sheet   85
10. Detail list   86
11. Major accidents to cleaners (2003–6)   97
12. Major causes of trip and slip accidents   97
13. Method statement for office cleaning   109
14. Job sheet   161

PREFACE

I would like to thank you personally for choosing to purchase my book. I do hope you find it both inspirational and useful. My personal experience of running a cleaning business may not apply to every such business, but I have done my best to approach the book from both a universal and individual point of view.

Becoming self-employed is an eye-opening and invigorating journey: you will experience highs and lows and will grow personally in ways you did not expect. You will learn more from being self-employed than any other job could ever teach you. Your success and destiny are in your own hands and, if you take anything from this book that will help you, the purpose of writing it has been fulfilled.

I wish you luck.

1
WORKING IN THE CLEANING INDUSTRY

❝ *Faith is taking the first step even when you don't see the whole staircase* ❞

(Martin Luther King, civil rights leader)

This chapter looks at the cleaning industry in general. Its aims are to give you an initial feel of the scale of the industry and to highlight some of the key issues and problems that are experienced in this sector.

Industry facts

The UK cleaning industry is huge. Current estimates show that it employs approximately 820,000 people and is worth somewhere in the region of £10 billion. It is a booming industry because cleaning services are in high demand and are considered a necessity. For this reason, the cleaning industry is generally immune from economic downturns.

Cleaning is a diverse industry covering everything from one cleaner with a couple of domestic properties to maintain each week to large commercial businesses with hundreds of staff on their books. There are also domestic cleaning staff, office cleaning staff, and hospital and school cleaning staff, not to mention the other niche sectors of the industry, such as carpet, window and vehicle cleaning. This book is mainly concerned with the provision of cleaning staff for commercial premises. With this in mind, the following are some of the basic statistics about the UK cleaning industry:

- ☐ There are approximately 30,000 businesses providing cleaning services at any given time.

- ☐ A third of all businesses are operated on a sole trader basis.

- ☐ Some 95% of these businesses employ 25 people or fewer, mainly in the following roles: management, administration, supervision and cleaning.

- ☐ Approximately 75% of the workforce are female and work only part time (between 10 and 16 hours per week).

- ☐ Some 65% of the workforce is over 40 years of age.

- ☐ Up to 20% of the workforce comes from ethnic minority backgrounds.

☐ It is estimated that 65% of the workforce has basic skills needs.

☐ On average, the industry experiences a 70% annual turnover of staff, equating to a retention rate of only 17 weeks.

What does this short summary tell us about the cleaning services industry? First, we can see that there are a lot of businesses and it is therefore true to say that cleaning is a competitive market. It is also true to say that 95% of the smaller businesses in the sector are either not growing or are simply merely surviving. It can also been seen from the above that the cleaning industry must be worth billions each year and, what is more, you don't require any specific qualifications to get started in the industry.

In short, this is why people choose to become involved in the cleaning services industry but, all too often, these people are unprepared both physically and mentally to deal with the various aspects of starting, running and building a successful business. It's not easy to become successful – you must be prepared for the work involved. What you need are a range of key personal skills, plus the determination to succeed.

Recruiting and retaining staff

The industry is labour driven – it is all about the provision of services, and this means the provision of staff to carry out these services. Research carried out by the Cleaning Industry National Training Organization (CINTO) found that the employment and retention of staff is the single biggest issue the industry has to deal with. Some of the findings of this research are summarized below:

☐ The cleaning industry workforce is predominately made up of females over the age of 40, mainly working part time.

☐ The workforce mostly comprises unqualified employees with basic skills needs.

☐ Some 90% of employers report difficulties in recruiting part-time staff, partly because of the pay and conditions and hours of work.

☐ Due to the very poor retention rates across the sector, the operatives who do remain in a job for more than a few months often find themselves quickly promoted to team leader or supervisor, without additional training or qualifications. Those in supervisory jobs are thus often weak in key skills, especially communication skills and application of number skills.

The recruitment and retention of staff, therefore, is seen as a key issue for the industry's future and, remember, it is people like the above whom you'll be employing.

Basic skills

Further research carried out by CINTO on behalf of the Basic Skills Agency tried to establish the impact of poor basic skills on the sector. The investigation addressed the importance of basic skills to the work undertaken. All the groups interviewed were asked whether basic skills really is an issue in the cleaning industry or whether workers can be effective in their jobs without the need to read, write, count or communicate to a significant level. While recognizing that the industry overlaps with other sectors, including manufacturing and sales, particular attention was given to the work done by the cleaning operatives themselves. It is fair to say that basic skills, as with all training, was not seen as an important issue for small to medium-sized enterprises where cleaning staff are sometimes transient and are not always viewed as an investment.

There is a common consensus that there are a number of tasks that require a basic level of competency in at least four areas:

1. **Reading**: health and safety notices; procedure documents; information regarding subcontractors; messages from clients; risk assessment documents and instructions; following directions to sites.

2. **Writing**: messages to clients; information and reports to managers and supervisors; orders for materials.

3. **Numbers**: cost control and the correct use of cleaning materials; the calculation of dilution ratios; the submission of time sheets for wage calculations; understanding the frequencies of cleaning.

4. **Communication**: the need to converse and communicate with clients and colleagues; understanding that contact should be made if unable to come to work; the passing on of information regarding problems.

Filling the skills gaps in the cleaning sector

Skills gaps are widely perceived to be more of a problem for operatives than for supervisory or management staff. Operatives often lack basic skills (for example, in reading and understanding health and safety procedures and regulations and in following instructions) as well as job-specific skills. Supervisory staff, on the other hand, are often deficient in communication skills, general supervisory skills and client service skills, while managers lack supervisory, general management and financial control skills.

Of those surveyed, 30% felt that their organization was affected by basic skills problems once a day or more often. The most common problem caused by this lack of basic skills involved understanding instructions. Some 4.8% of employers believed they had staff who lacked a basic competency in English (these employees represent 4.9% of the workforce). This information has been confirmed by CINTO, who added that listening to instructions is an additional problem.

Qualifications

The following qualifications are applicable to the cleaning industry:

- □ National Vocational Qualification (NVQ) Levels 1 and 2 Cleaning and Support Services.

- □ NVQ Levels 1 and 2 Cleaning Building Interiors.

- □ NVQ Level 2 Caretaking.

- □ NVQ Level 2 Cleaning (Windows, Glass and Façade Services; Within Food Premises; and On-site Care of Carpets and Soft Furnishings).

- □ British Institute of Cleaning Science (BICSc) Certificate of Cleaning Science (in conjunction with City and Guilds (C&G)).

- □ BICSc Certificate of Cleaning Services Supervision (in conjunction with C&G).

There are currently some 35,000 staff who are qualified at NVQ Level 1, but only about 2,000 employees are working towards Level 2. Chris James at Asset Skills (www.assetskills.org/site) suggests that the NVQ Level 1 Cleaning Building Interiors qualification is appropriate for the cleaning industry, as are all the mandatory units for Level 2 (the Cleaning and Support Services, Cleaning Building Interiors and Caretaking NVQs are all mapped out on the Department for Education and Skills' website – see www.dfes.gov.uk/readwriteplus/nosmapping/tree/fa00/nvq00305/).

The BICSc certificate is a practical, competency-based test that comprises some 40 units. Candidates (or, more usually, their employers) select the competencies they need. The assessment process is not as rigorous as the NVQ, relying instead on a one-off assessment of practical performance. No level has been allocated to this qualification.

To sum up, therefore:

- □ Some 50% of those employed in the cleaning industry have no qualifications and, within this workforce, only 10.6% of employees have a competency-based cleaning qualification.

- □ The most popular qualification appears to be BICSc (7.3%), followed by S/NVQ (3.8%).

- □ Just over 11% of employees are working towards a qualification (of these, 5.8% are working towards BICSc and 3.8% towards S/NVQ).

- □ Level 1 is the most common qualification. While Level 3 qualifications for younger people receive the bulk of public funding, the priority for the industry are lower-level qualifications for older people.

- □ Of employers, 62% consider it very important to improve their employees' basic skills, but employers are often reluctant to release their staff for long-term training due to the financial implications.

□ Finally, most employees who undertake training do so on a 'day release' basis, and some employees fund their own training.

The priority areas for skills development in the sector, therefore, appear to be as follows:

□ Reading and understanding job and safety instructions.

□ Reading and understanding health and safety procedures and regulations.

□ Communicating with a range of people.

□ Measuring cleaning fluids accurately.

□ Completing simple workplace documentation.

Dealing with the franchise problem

Franchising is a very popular way of starting up in business: those people who are concerned about their expertise in a specific business area appreciate the security a franchise can offer because they are buying into what is already a successful business model and there are no sales requirements or the need to find new clients.

While franchises are undoubtedly successful and many people are satisfied with their current franchise arrangements, the problem remains, however, that, when you become self-employed and start to run your own cleaning business, one of your main goals – if not *the* main goal – will be to make as much money as you can and to live comfortably. If this is the case, you must ask yourself this: once you are established and are confident in running your own business, will you be happy to share all your hard-earned profits with someone else for the remainder of the time you will be self-employed?

As a businessman or woman, this question is important because, as a franchisee, you will be paying a percentage of your earnings back to your franchisor each month and every month and, in most cases, there will be various other fees to pay, such as:

□ the initial investment and intellectual property fees;

□ monthly royalties on net turnover – generally 10–15%;

□ advertising and marketing fees; and

□ management fees.

All these small sums will chip away at your profit each and every month. The following is an example of what can happen.

CASE STUDY

Mr Aslam was interested in running a cleaning business but was unsure if he had the skills to start up alone. He decided to purchase a franchise and had a meeting with a franchise company who seemed to be market leaders in cleaning franchising. Mr Aslam opted to purchase an initial turnover of £8,000 per month of net business. This meant the franchisor would be obliged to provide this level of business (e.g. eight cleaning accounts at £1,000 plus VAT per month). The cost of this franchise would be £3 for every £1 of business supplied so, this level of business would cost Mr Aslam an initial purchase price of £24,000. He also has an intellectual property (IP) fee to pay to buy into the franchise which varies, depending on the quantity of business purchased. In our example the purchase level of business is £24,000, and this falls into the IP bracket of a further £15,000. So Mr Aslam will have purchased a franchise for a total price of £39,000 and will, in turn, be provided with £8,000 per month of business. Seems straightforward, doesn't it?

However, consider the following. The franchisor will more than likely have a period of time to meet their obligation – anything up to three or possibly six months – before Mr Aslam receives the full £8,000 per month of business. Mr Aslam would be told that this is to ease him in slowly and, to a certain degree, this is a sound approach, but it can also be bad news. The franchisor may not have enough new sales coming in, and Mr Aslam may therefore have to wait for his business obligation. How would he supplement his income during this period?

In addition, if after receiving his full obligation Mr Aslam lost any of his accounts, then he would have to pay to replace them. The principle here is that, if it were deemed Mr Aslam's fault that an account was lost, then this would come off his obligation and would only be replaced at extra cost to himself. Remember, commercial cleaning is a high-churn business – accounts can and will be cancelled for various reasons. Sometimes, clients will find fault with the cleaning simply as a means to cancel a contract: perhaps they are experiencing financial difficulties or a better offer is available. Let's look at the effect this can have.

Some 12 months have passed, and Mr Aslam has finally reached his obligation of £8,000 per month of business. It was slow coming and he struggled for a few months, but he finally got there. He is also now much more settled and is becoming familiar with the ins and outs of the industry and is ready to grow his business further. In the next two months, however, three of his accounts cancel, citing that they have had a few problems throughout the year and that they feel a change is good idea. Despite his best efforts, these accounts cancel, and the franchisor deems them to be 'performance related' cancellations that will be deducted from the obligation.

Mr Aslam now has only £5,000 of business per month and no further obligation to receive. He can, of course, ask for more business from the franchisor, but this would cost him either further bulk costs or ever-higher increased percentages to pay back each month.

Two years have now passed, and Mr Aslam has taken on a further £5,000 worth of business with the franchisor, despite the extra costs. He is beginning to make a go of things: he is now at a level of £10,000 per month of business and employs 19 cleaning staff. Two of his original obligation clients have complained to the franchisor as opposed to Mr Aslam, who could have dealt with the problems himself. The franchisor sent an account manager to deal with the complaints and charged Mr Aslam for this. The franchisor then deemed that these accounts posed a strong cancellation risk. Because of this risk, they removed the accounts from Mr Aslam and transferred them to another franchisee to ensure they retained these clients. A further £2,000 of obligation is therefore now lost, bringing the obligation total down to £3,000. Not only that, but also another franchisee has had to pay to take on the two new accounts, which Mr Aslam has already paid for and which are now lost!

Three years have now passed and lessons have been learnt. Mr Aslam is feeling a bit despondent about his franchising experience but, on the positive side, he is now extremely confident in the running of his franchise, he has learnt from losing these accounts and he has really raised his game and is running his business very well. His clients love him, his staff are happy and he has taken on a further £10,000 of business from his franchisor, which is now at a level of £18,000 per month. All in all, he is now well and truly up and running and is growing his business.

Herein lies the next problem. It has been three years now, and Mr Aslam knows the industry extremely well. He is looking to grow his business but the franchisor has been experiencing difficulty in finding new sales in his region and there are also other franchisees locally waiting in line for new business. Nothing is on the horizon, so that means no growth for the foreseeable future and, considering the high churn rate of cleaning accounts, this spells trouble.

Mr Aslam is confident, however – he has leads to bring in further business himself, which the franchisor welcomes. Over a three-month period he brings in a further £3,000 of business, the royalties from which he will still pay to the franchisor who, as they always do, will invoice his clients direct and will collect all monies and make all deductions before passing the remainder to Mr Aslam. Just over three years have passed and Mr Aslam's turnover is £21,000 per month, some of which has been generated by Mr Aslam himself. Taking into account all the fees per month, an average of 15% is being returned to the franchisor every month: £3,150 per month is being deducted as fees and royalties.

To repeat the question posed earlier in this chapter: once you are established and are confident in running your own business, will you be happy to share all your hard-earned profits with someone else for the remainder of the time you will be self-employed? I think not! The sum of it is, you will become confident in and familiar with your business, you will eventually grow out of needing a franchisor to assist you and you will start to think about the £x,xxx per month you are 'losing'. You will then begin to think about the £y,yyy per month you will be 'losing' should your turnover double – and so on!

The obvious choice is to quit the franchise and to set up exclusively on your own, but what about that franchise agreement you signed that, on reflection, is water tight and has you completely over a barrel? It is, of course, there to protect the franchisor, and they have every right to this protection but, as standard, you will have signed to say that for a period of *x* amount of years after you leave the franchise you will not run or be deemed to be involved in the running of any business that could be construed as being in competition with your franchisor, and you will also have signed to say that you cannot approach any of 'their' clients. In other words, it turns out that all those clients you have been slogging your guts over to keep happy for the past three years are not actually yours at all – they never have been, in fact.

The above case study is typical of what can happen, but in other cases people have lost many thousands of pounds and have walked away from a franchise with nothing at all. Be under no illusions – this does happen. My advice is, and always will be, to stay away from commercial cleaning franchises. Franchises are businesses looking to make money just like you, and they will play hard ball at your expense if and when required.

If you have the ambition and the will to succeed and if you can utilize the tools provided in this book, then choose to go it alone: you will make it. In the event you don't make it, then consider that, in a franchised situation, you will have lost a large sum of money that will never be returned.

Thinking positively

This book does not purport that cleaning is the greatest business in the world and that there are nothing but good things to come out of it. If it did then it would not only be doing you a disservice but it would also be a waste of your money. The fact is that cleaning is a hard business to run and to get right. The same goes for any business – everyone would be successful if it was that easy. With this is mind you can expect to read things in this book that may put you off even from starting a cleaning business in the first place. Whatever decision you eventually make, it is important that you are aware of the good, bad and ugly sides of running a cleaning business.

If you do feel put off by this, take a minute to come back to this section and read the following:

☐ Cleaning can and will make you a lot of money.

☐ No business is easy to run – period!

☐ Cleaning is a regular 'bread and butter' business – money is constantly coming in.

☐ You will be your own boss – there is no one to answer to but yourself.

☐ Cleaning is a very flexible business to run.

☐ You will find great staff who are a pleasure to work with.

☐ You will make good relationships with clients and develop friendships.

☐ Becoming successful brings confidence and the respect of others.

☐ Every self-employed person complains about their business or industry but they almost always finish by saying it is better than working for someone else.

☐ Your destiny is in your own hands.

2

DECIDING BETWEEN THE
VARIOUS CLEANING SERVICES

Destiny is no matter of chance. It is a matter of choice. It is not a thing to be waited for, it is a thing to be achieved

(William Jenning Bry, American politician, orator and lawyer)

As you have seen, cleaning is a large and diverse industry. This book, however, is primarily concerned with daily cleaning services, and this chapter looks at the various areas of cleaning provision you are likely to experience and come to provide as your business grows.

Daily cleaning services are the best way to start your business. The reason for this is that you will have a bread-and-butter income – there is no point in focusing your efforts on letting agency cleans or builders' cleans because these are not required on a daily basis in the same way as office cleaning, for example. Daily cleans are also needed in offices, pubs and schools throughout the country, and this will be your core business and will ensure that, each month, you have a steady flow of income.

Cleaning offices

In terms of daily cleaning provision, office cleaning is where you want to be. Office cleaning is the target sector for most daily cleaning companies and, because of this, it is a competitive area to be in. The key benefits of office cleaning can be summarized as follows:

☐ It generally involves Monday to Friday cleans only.

☐ The cleaning required is on a much lighter scale than in cinemas and pubs, etc.

☐ The cleaning is normally done outside normal working hours.

☐ There are opportunities for additional business through companies that have additional offices or through recommendations.

☐ It is easier to find good staff for office cleaning than for other types of cleaning.

If you are able to build up a good level of business in office cleaning, you will have the benefit of being able to switch off at the weekends when most offices are not open – a luxury that will not be afforded to you should you be cleaning for seven-day businesses, such as pubs, clubs and cinemas. Depending on how active and hands on you choose to be, you will also find that you will be busy early in the morning to late morning, and then late in the afternoon to early evening. It should be added, however, that this 'leisure' time should be spent finding new clients, but the point remains that you will be relatively quiet during the middle of the day.

When you have had the experience of cleaning a cinema on a Sunday morning with two cleaning staff short, you will quickly realize the benefits of an office clean: an office clean will never compare with the dirt levels experienced in cinemas. Office cleaning, generally speaking, covers the following basic areas:

☐ Desktops and surfaces cleaned.

☐ Floors vacuumed or mopped.

☐ Waste baskets emptied.

☐ Kitchens cleaned.

☐ Toilets cleaned.

☐ Glass cleaning and other small duties.

Cleaning staff generally prefer to clean out of hours because they can work more quickly and efficiently than in a busy office. It also avoids complaints about the vacuum being on while someone is on the phone or the problems of cleaning a toilet of the opposite sex when someone needs to come in to use it. Out-of-hours cleans are also useful when you have key access. For example, a member of the cleaning staff might call in sick at short notice and, because you have the keys, you can go in slightly later (if this is allowed) with a replacement cleaner to ensure the shift is covered.

Office cleaning presents other opportunities. You may, for example, have a client who has two other branches locally and who, no doubt, will also be receiving a cleaning service which you would like to become involved in. This is where the value of good service and good relations with your clients comes in to play: they will be only too happy to recommend you when the office manager of their other office mentions they are unhappy with their current service provider and that they would like to change companies.

More often than not, you will get better staff and better consistency if you undertake office cleaning and, just like yourself, you will find that your cleaning staff also enjoy the weekend off. You will get far more 'sickies' at weekends than you will during a normal working week, so the balance is generally better and staff relations will remain good.

Cleaning pubs and leisure premises

We all know what pubs are, but what does 'leisure premises' cover? Leisure cleans are generally represented by the following types of premises:

☐ restaurants

☐ cinemas

- ☐ health clubs

- ☐ bowling alleys

- ☐ nightclubs

- ☐ casinos.

All the above (including pubs) are normally seven-day cleans, and some require cleaning at unsociable hours.

Pub and leisure cleaning accounts are easier to come by than office cleans because the churn rate is normally higher in pub and leisure cleaning. This means that such clients are on the lookout for cleaning companies more often than office cleaning clients. There are a number of reasons for these high churn rates for pub and leisure accounts, some of which are as follows:

- ☐ This industry is extremely competitive, and the managers take a very active role in the cleaning.

- ☐ Such businesses are generally audited by a department of their own company, which scores them on a number of factors – cleaning being one of them.

- ☐ They are constantly trying to reduce overheads due to the competitive nature of the market.

- ☐ They change managers more frequently than offices, and these changes can have a roll-on effect on subcontractors and service providers.

- ☐ It is more difficult to find good staff willing to work in these areas.

The big pub chains are in a constant battle with each other for customers. They are obliged to have the cleanest and best facilities as well as the best deals on alcohol, with good food and a good service that will attract customers. This is why they are relentless when it comes to pushing their own staff to strive for results and to reduce overheads, and it is only a matter of time before the cleaning overheads will be looked at. On a whim, new company policy could be that they will now employ their own cleaning staff to reduce costs.

When this happens, the natural step is that they will approach your cleaning staff, seeking to employ them directly and thus cutting you out of the picture. This often happens and, even though it does not make the manager's job any easier, it will improve their figures – it is, after all, about results and performance.

Because of the pressures managers are under, there are always changes in management, particularly in pubs. Sometimes this can work in your favour. For example, a manager who is your client may move to another pub and you may get to provide the services there while retaining the existing account at the previous pub. The reverse, however, can happen: you may lose out completely when a manager you are used to dealing with leaves or moves elsewhere but does not take you with them.

There will also be pressure from you towards your cleaning staff because of the pressure you receive to meet your client's standards. Unfortunately, cleaning staff do not take too well to pressure for what, to them, is only a couple of hours a day part-time income. They will resent having to deal with constant criticism and also with having to work weekends, particularly when they can get an office cleaning job with less hassle and weekends off. Regular staff changes are commonplace in this type of work.

Overall, therefore, you will find not only that the cleaning is more difficult in terms of general dirt levels but also that the managers of such premises will be far more involved in and critical of the cleaning. You will also have difficulty in getting good, reliable staff, and you will not make as good margins as you would through office cleaning.

To finish on a positive note, pub cleaning will give you a good, all-round education about daily cleaning – you will be hands on and it will provide you with high levels of service that will be of benefit to you in your core office-cleaning work. There will be plenty of opportunities to pick up pub cleaning accounts when you first launch your business, and you will learn a great deal from the audit process and from your clients, which can only help you as you move forward. I say this with experience!

Builders' cleans

Builders' cleans should sit well with your daily cleaning business, and you should definitely find the time to market yourself to building companies. The reason they fit well with daily cleaning is that most builders' cleans are carried out during the middle of the day. However, if the client requires cleaning during a specific time, then you will have to meet this request. Most of the time, though, you should be able to dictate the time to suit your own requirements.

You should pitch your builders' cleaning time to between 9.30 a.m. and 3.30 p.m. The reason for this is that you will already have a number of cleaning staff working for you in the early morning and early evening. Daytime cleaning will not only give you the opportunity to offer your staff additional work but will also provide you with cleaning staff whom you know can do the job well. Most of your morning cleans should finish around 9 a.m., and the earliest of your evening cleans should start at about 4 p.m.

Clients tend to have their own phrases to describe the type of clean they require, so if they use any of the following terms to describe the clean simply adopt that term and use it to head your quote:

☐ final cleans

☐ handover cleans

- □ sparkle cleans

- □ finishing cleans

- □ deep cleans.

Some clients will frown if their 'sparkle clean' is referred to as a 'builders' clean' because 'builders' clean' suggests a lower standard of finish. With experience you will soon pick up the correct terminology.

All these cleans (including builders' cleans) will, in most cases, cover the following types of work and/or premises:

- □ new-build homes

- □ new-build commercial premises

- □ letting agencies

- □ shopfitters

- □ refurbishments

- □ office moves.

Cleaning new-build homes

On completion, all new-build homes require a finishing clean, and a cleaning company is generally employed to carry this out. It is not enough simply to send a mailshot to the house builder as, more often than not, the builder will be a large company and your mailshot will be ignored. You should spend time in advance finding out the name of the person or department who deals with this aspect of the building process and you should send your details directly to them. Generally speaking, the people involved will be the surveyors or site managers.

The benefits of this type of work are that it pays more and that, if you are successful, you will be able to obtain some advance contracted work for future new developments. There is nothing better than having future work on your books.

Cleaning new-build commercial premises

New-build commercial premises are similar to the above but are generally carried out by a different type of building company. All the above, therefore, applies to new-build commercial premises, but there are a few other things you should also bear in mind. Some of these things are vitally important, not only if you are to get this type of work but also if you are to make money from it:

- □ All your staff will have to have the appropriate personal protective equipment (PPE) when on site (i.e. hard hats, yellow vests and proper footwear).

☐ In most cases you will need 110 V equipment because building sites do not have a normal 240 V supply until after handover.

☐ You will have to have a recognized supervisor on site who will liaise with the site manager or other nominated person.

☐ You will need to build into your quote that the price covers 'one clean only plus any snagging per area' and 'that any repeat cleans caused by other subcontractors' messes are chargeable'.

The last point is important. In the lead-up to the handover date, everyone will be falling over everyone else's feet to get the job completed on time: cleaning staff, subcontractors and labourers alike. Without doubt, that nice room your staff have just cleaned will be revisited by a pair of mucky builders' boots while someone else finishes off a bit of painting, fixes a loose handle, etc. Toilets are a classic example of this – the last subcontractors in are the mastic contractors, and they will make a mess.

In terms of a quote price, you should calculate your expected man hours from your site visit and then add 10% to cover extras, applying a rate of approximately £10–£12 per hour. This will keep you competitive and should also return a decent profit.

You may have to become Construction Industry Scheme registered in order to work for these companies. There is a Construction Industry Scheme card that is relatively easy to obtain by contacting HM Revenue & Customs.

Finally, make a point of chasing your payment promptly after 30 days – the big building companies are notoriously slow payers and, in some cases, you will be kept waiting for 90 days or more. Chase your payment through the various departments until it gets to accounts payable, and then ask for a payment date and follow up accordingly.

Domestic cleans

Domestic cleaning is a huge part of the industry and, like all the other sectors, it has its advantages and disadvantages. It is up to you whether or not you want to become involved in this side of the industry, either as your main focus or as part of the wider range of services you offer. Domestic cleans are usually categorized as follows. Cleaning provision for:

☐ homeowners

☐ letting agencies

☐ housing associations.

CLEANING FOR HOMEOWNERS

Domestic cleaning is a significant slice of the overall industry. Current estimates suggest that domestic cleaning is worth £3 billion per year in the UK and that the sector is continuing to grow. You will possibly have seen adverts for Molly Maid or Merry Maid who are both big players in domestic cleaning. They are both also franchised operations – most national domestic-cleaning companies are franchised.

One reason this sector is growing is that more and more people have demanding careers – women as well as men. There is also more disposable income now, and people are less inclined to clean their own homes. It is reasons such as these that have caused the domestic cleaning industry to mushroom.

You will have to carry out some local market research to identify the target homeowners who may require this service. For example:

□ upper/middle-class professionals

□ young executives and professionals

□ affluent elderly people.

The easiest way to attract business initially is leaflet drops. As your business grows, you could advertise in local newspapers and *Yellow Pages*. You should also pick up further business by word of mouth. If you have branded your business (see Chapter 3), you may also have a car or small van with advertising on it: no opportunity should be missed to advertise for new business.

One thing to avoid is to try to cover too wide an area too soon. Unlike office or pub cleaning, you will have to provide your staff with transport to move them from one job to another. As you expand, you should consider the cost of vehicles and fuel – it certainly wouldn't be cost effective to send your staff across the country and back again, so do try to keep your target area fairly compact.

As with all other cleaning services, selecting the right staff is very important. For domestic cleaning, two members of staff working as a team is normal. These people will usually go from job to job, but you must make sure that service levels don't suffer from staff rushing to get through a certain number of jobs on any given day. As with most of the cleaning services discussed in this chapter, you should be prepared to roll up your sleeves and to get involved in the work, if required.

As you would expect, homeowners will be concerned about the staff you provide as these people may well have access to someone's home when the homeowner is not there. In this way domestic cleaning is far more personal than office cleaning, for example. This is not, however, always a good thing because people are far more sensitive about their homes than about their place of work.

One of the biggest benefits of domestic cleaning is that it is a cash-positive business: in most cases you will be paid on a weekly basis in cash or by cheque, which will be an enormous help with your running costs.

CLEANING FOR LETTING AGENCIES

Letting agencies (and property management companies, etc.) employ cleaning companies on a regular basis. While these types of cleans are not sufficient for you to build your business on, they might be considered as add-ons.

Letting agency cleans differ from homeowner cleans in the following ways:

☐ They are mainly one-off cleans as opposed to weekly or monthly cleans.

☐ The properties are generally empty.

☐ Some properties may be completely trashed.

☐ Deep cleans are normally required as a minimum.

☐ The location of premises will vary greatly.

☐ Time will be required to pick up and return keys to the agencies.

☐ The work can be at very short notice.

☐ Complaints may arise that need to be attended to immediately.

☐ Agencies are driven by price, so you will need to be competitive.

☐ There are longer waiting periods for payment.

Depending on how efficient your cleaning staff are, what you charge for your work will appear to be highly competitive, but this type of work is, in fact, quite profitable. The reasons for this are the various property sizes and the requirements for one-off cleans. As you would expect, a two-bedroom flat will require less cleaning time than a four-bedroom house. On the other hand, a completely trashed two-bedroom flat could possibly take longer to clean than a four-bedroom house that only requires a light clean.

There is no hard and fast way of knowing exactly how long it will take to clean each property you are offered. In a perfect world you would clean the property and then charge the client after the clean was over when you knew the labour time involved. Unless you have a very good relationship with your contact in the agency, there is little chance the agent will risk this method of working because it could obviously be abused financially.

The answer to this problem is to put together some sort of pricing matrix that will cover both light and deep cleans for all sizes of property. In addition, you should include the costs of all the extra services the letting agent may require. In the pricing matrix shown in Figure 1 on page 18, the prices given are an example only – every area of the country has its own prices.

If you are able to charge these prices for the different sizes of property listed, on most occasions you will yield much higher profit margins than you would for general office

Domestic Cleaning & Services Tariff

Property Size	Light Clean	Deep Clean
1 Bedroom	£55.00	£115.00
2 Bedrooms	£75.00	£135.00
3 Bedrooms	£95.00	£155.00
4 Bedrooms	£115.00	£175.00
5 Bedrooms	£135.00	£195.00
6 Bedrooms	£155.00	£215.00

The above prices include all internal window cleaning

Carpet & Upholstery Cleaning	
This service is a commercial deep-extraction clean using deodorizers and microbiological inhibitors	
First carpet up to 20 sq m	£40.00
Additional carpets	£25.00
Suite – up to 5 seats	£75.00
Additional seats	£15.00
Rugs – on-site	£30.00
Rugs – off-site	£42.00
Carpet stain guarding	£1.50 per sq m
Upholstery stain guarding	£13.00 per seat
Curtains	£7.00 per sq m
Stain removal call-out charge	£40.00

Additional Services		
External window cleaning	Minimum charge £25.00 up to 5 windows – £3.00 per extra window	
Lamp replacements	Halogens – £4.00 each	Bayonet 40w – £2.50 each
Rubbish disposal	£4.50 per black bag of rubbish removed and disposed	
On-site skip service	£250.00 – skip plus labourer for one day to fill skip	
Full electrical service	£29.00 for first hour – £24.00 per hour thereafter	
Plumbing repairs	£25.00 for first hour – £15.00 per hour thereafter	
General maintenance	£25.00 for first hour – £15.00 per hour thereafter	
Room painting 'touch ups'	Patch paint to freshen rooms – £60 per room, including paint	
Full decoration service	Price on request	
Flooring and carpets	Price on request	
Specialist services	Price on request	

Fig. 1 Pricing matrix

cleaning. For example, a two-bedroom, light-clean flat could easily be cleaned in three to four hours. (You will notice at the bottom of this matrix a list of trade services, such as electrical, plumbing and painting. These services are optional and are covered in more depth in Chapter 14.)

CLEANING FOR HOUSING ASSOCIATIONS

There are only a few small differences between cleaning provision for letting agencies and housing associations. First, and from a positive point of view, housing associations have huge numbers of properties in closely knit areas. Not only this, but there are also additional cleaning services that can be supplied for the common areas most housing associations take responsibility for. For example:

☐ refuse areas

☐ foyers

☐ stairwells

☐ entrances.

The company that takes care of house cleans and clearances usually looks after the communal areas as well.

Secondly, and negatively, it is far more difficult to pick up housing association cleans than letting agency cleans. In most big cities, for example, there are likely to be far more letting agencies than housing associations, and there are also likely to be many experienced cleaning companies with better contacts than you who are in a much stronger position to pick this work up. Depending on what type of a person you are, this fact will either put you off completely or inspire you to get yourself into the position where you can obtain this work.

For most of the larger housing associations, you will be required to apply to become an approved contractor. You should therefore request an application pack to initiate the process of becoming approved. Once approved, your position as an approved contractor will usually be reviewed annually. Fill in the application pack carefully – you do not want to rule yourself out of the running before your application is even considered by the decision-making panel. Some of the problems that may affect you are as follows. You may be required to:

☐ provide managed accounts for your business for the past few years;

☐ have a much larger level of insurance cover than you would normally require;

☐ provide health and safety records;

☐ show that you are registered with certain bodies (such as the International Organization for Standardization – ISO); and/or

☐ provide cash projections for your business.

In other words, you will be required to give an arm and a leg and to spend a great deal of time and perhaps money to complete and submit an application that could still be rejected.

Finally, housing associations are one of the worst types of client when it comes to price. Most housing associations are under-funded and are constantly required to save money left, right and centre wherever they can. You will certainly not receive your desired rates from housing associations but, to finish on a positive note, if you do manage to get in and to prove yourself, you will have a very good client who will provide you with a large amount of consistent work over a long period of time. Sometimes this fact alone is enough to warrant the effort of becoming an approved provider of cleaning services to housing associations.

It is ultimately up to you to decided what type of domestic cleaning service you will provide. The following are some final tips on domestic cleaning that may help you to make your decision:

☐ **Staff quality**: the importance of having good staff cannot be emphasized enough. Try to build a team of reliable, discrete workers who have a good attitude towards their work. This is never easy, but you won't even get off the ground without the right people behind you.

☐ **Staff turnover**: you should be prepared to have a high staff turnover. While you will make mistakes yourself, your cleaning staff will have the habit of letting you down. Therefore only take on people recommended to you by existing, good-quality staff.

☐ **Criticism**: make sure your cleaning staff are aware from the start that criticism is par for the course and that they will sometimes have to deal with difficult people. Hopefully, when the problems are at their worst, your staff will be able to deal with them.

☐ **Satisfaction**: keeping customers satisfied is of paramount importance, but it is wise to remember that satisfied staff are equally as important. If you have good staff, do all you can to ensure they are happy and satisfied when in your employment.

☐ **Financial balance**: you will always be looking for opportunities to obtain the highest possible amount from your customers and, likewise, you will not be keen to pay over the odds to your cleaning staff: the bit in the middle is your profit, after all. Remember, however, that higher prices mean fewer clients and that lower wages mean fewer staff who are willing to work for you. Find the balance that is right for you.

☐ **Consistency**: clients love nothing more than consistency. Where possible, send the same cleaning staff at the same time and on the same day, unless otherwise requested. Clients become unsettled very easily and, if this can be avoided with a managed consistency, all the better.

☐ **Versatility**: adapting to your clients' needs is very important. Every client will want something different, so it is important to take a personal approach to each one in order to accommodate their individual needs. A one-size-fits-all service isn't the answer!

Window cleaning

While window cleaning can be a business in its own right, it is considered here as an addition to your core service of daily cleaning provision. There is, of course, nothing to say that, as you develop your cleaning business and add more and more window cleaning accounts, you might want to consider window cleaning as your core business. The choice will ultimately be yours but, in this section, we will look at this type of cleaning service in general and will examine some of its pros and cons.

Window cleaning is very worthwhile. Consider the following:

☐ It is extremely profitable.

☐ A window cleaning business can be run successfully by one person only.

☐ The knowledge required is basic and simple to learn.

☐ Little investment is required to get a business up and running.

☐ Very little storage space is required.

☐ It is a service that is constantly required in both small towns and large cities.

☐ It is cash positive.

As you will have noticed, there are many positives about window cleaning.

There are three ways you can provide a window cleaning service to your clients:

1. **Do the cleaning yourself.** *Positives*: you will be able to assure the quality of your service and you will be able to protect your clients from being poached. You will also be able to learn the techniques and time involved, which will help you to price your work. *Negatives*: you will be spending your time cleaning windows, not concentrating on the overall growth and development of your business.

2. **Subcontract to an existing window cleaning company**. *Positives*: an experienced service provider will carry out the work and you will have no financial commitments to the contractor other than for the work provided. You will also have more free time to concentrate on developing your business. *Negatives*: your profit margins will be reduced, and there is always the possibility the contractor will poach your clients or vice versa. You also have less control over a contractor.

3. **Employ someone directly to carry out the work**. *Positives*: your profits will be higher and you can control the window cleaner and the work. You will have time to concentrate on developing your business. *Negatives*: you may employ an inexperienced or poor window cleaner who will reflect badly on your business. You are also committed to finding work to cover your employee's wages.

The choice, as always, is yours. It is, however, best initially to subcontract the work to someone who is reliable, consistent and trustworthy. Don't initially concern yourself with high profit margins but concentrate on the quality of the service as this will assist growth. When you have enough business, employ someone part time and also keep the subcontractor on-board. This will give you the time to assess and train the employee before you cancel your subcontractor. If all goes well, you will eventually remove the subcontractor and carry out the work yourself, thereby increasing your profits and securing your position against the poaching of clients, etc.

A further choice is whether to undertake commercial work only or to combine commercial work with domestic window cleaning. Depending on your staffing levels, from both a window cleaner and management point of view, ideally you should do both to take advantage of all the available business. Domestic window cleaning comprises sole traders, so you may find it difficult to penetrate this sector as a larger company managing not just window cleaning but also all the other cleaning services you offer.

The following are some tips for domestic window cleaning, should you decide to give it a go:

☐ Establish both a regular route and a frequency of cleans per client.

☐ Use your route to pick up other clients in the area.

☐ Concentrate on providing regular window-washing services for all the one and two-storey office buildings and shop fronts in your area, as well as your domestic cleans.

☐ Start with those closest to your home or office and expand your efforts outwards.

☐ Choose busy thoroughfares in which to target clients because this will mean more cleans in a shorter period of time, resulting in higher profits.

☐ Act on the complaints clients may have and always leave a leaflet or business card because they may come back to you later.

☐ Try to maintain your professional approach and provide quotes in writing or via email whenever you can – verbal prices suit some clients, but this is a less professional approach.

☐ Be competitive and undercut competitors if necessary, using not only price but also any other benefits you can offer.

☐ Be wary of undercutting, however, because this is not conducive to a good reputation and will also lessen your profit margins.

☐ Try not to take on too much too quickly – your quality of service will suffer for it.

☐ Move swiftly if potential clients call because you may find that they are simply going through a list of numbers and that the quickest reaction will get the work.

☐ Remember to ensure your quality service at all times. This must also be emphasized strongly to anyone you employ because they are your business's face.

□ Use good-quality cleaning materials and supplies.

A further point regarding commercial window-cleaning work is health and safety. Most city-centre offices involve high-level cleaning, and a ladder, therefore, is not always feasible. By law, these premises should have safety eye bolts that are periodically tested for any work or access that is required beyond the windows. If these are not in place, you should not carry out the work. Gone are the days when window cleaners perched on high ledges without support or harnessing of some type. Your cleaning staff (and subcontractors, for that matter) should enforce the use of safety harnesses and lanyards for high-level cleaning such as this. Risk assessments must be taken to ensure the safety of all the people concerned.

For external cleaning, you should also consider the more modern method of window cleaning – the reach and wash system. This is a van-mounted window cleaning system that uses a telescopic pole that can reach very high heights. The windows are cleaned by pure water fed through the extending pole, which can reach to heights of six floors.

Cleaning carpets and upholstery

Nearly all domestic and commercial properties have carpets, carpet tiles, rugs or upholstery of some kind. Instead of replacing these when they get dirty or stained, a cost-effective alternative is to have them cleaned professionally. To provide a carpet cleaning service to domestic or commercial clients, you will more than likely need some training. You will also need to invest in a variety of equipment. A great many of the larger manufacturers offer free training if you purchase your machinery and materials from them, so this is a good thing to look out for.

Like window cleaning, a carpet cleaning service is often started by someone who runs the business hands on before developing it and taking on employees. You will therefore need to look again at the three choices mentioned earlier when starting a window cleaning service – substituting 'carpet cleaning' for 'window cleaning', where appropriate.

Again, in the short term you should subcontract the work to allow you time to develop your business and so that you learn about the service fully from a technical and pricing point of view. You should perhaps also consider going on a carpet cleaning course that will help you to understand the service you are selling. These courses are generally one or two days and cost approximately £100–£200. On this course you will learn the following important things about carpet and upholstery cleaning:

□ Carpet construction and the cleaning methods for different types of carpet.

□ Carpet fibre identification.

□ Approved cleaning methods.

□ Stain removal techniques.

□ Protective treatments.

☐ Fabric cleaning.

☐ The wet and dry cleaning of upholstery, including leather.

☐ Carpet surveying.

☐ Job pricing.

☐ Selling techniques.

These are the basics – you will likely pick up a great deal more information besides. Most training schools also offer a course on hard-floor cleaning and maintenance, which is another service you may want to consider offering. To provide a professional carpet cleaning service, it is vital you are well trained because there are so many factors to consider to achieve the best possible result from a carpet, upholstery or rug clean. You will also obviously require a vehicle for transporting your equipment from job to job because this can be bulky and heavy.

Like all the other services discussed in this chapter, carpet and upholstery cleaning is a competitive market. You will need to make a strong push on advertising and marketing if you are to win business. Follow this with a professional, high-quality and well priced service, and you will soon build up repeat business while continuously adding new customers via word of mouth and advertising.

A final comment about equipment and chemicals. You do not need to buy every bit of kit recommended by a manufacturer's sales team – certainly not in the initial start-up period. Likewise, you do not need to buy large amounts of every chemical they produce. You should ask someone in the industry to give you some frank and unbiased advice about the 'core' equipment and chemicals you should carry. With experience you will be able to make your own decisions about which extra items you should add to your kit.

IT (information technology) and specialist cleans

IT cleaning is simply the provision of a cleaning service for IT equipment. This is purely a commercial service and is normally required either for hygiene reasons or because the equipment is sensitive or expensive and is located in a controlled environment.

The ideal situation is to establish a pattern of repeat scheduled cleaning visits, the normal pitch being that the follow-up cleans will be less expensive because the 'main' clean has already been carried out. This encourages the client to commit themselves to further cleans. Further selling points for this service are as follows:

☐ It improves hygiene, thus resulting in fewer staff absence days.

☐ It helps to protect the equipment.

☐ There is low work disruption during the service.

Equipment	Price per Item Cleaned
Monitors	£1.25
PC/base units	£1.45
Keyboards	£0.75
Mice	£0.50
Telephones	£0.95
Printers	£3.75
Fax machines	£3.75
Photocopiers	£4.75
Scanners	£2.75
Laptops	£2.45
Mobiles	£0.75
Pin machines	£0.95

Fig. 2. IT equipment cleaning price list

☐ It prevents the build-up of static electricity, which can cause static shocks.

☐ It optimizes equipment performance and reduces maintenance and replacement costs.

☐ The products used are biodegradable.

☐ The cleaning solutions will flash dry and can be used again almost immediately.

☐ The solutions are non-toxic to humans but can kill such viruses as MRSA.

The typical items to be cleaned in most offices include:

☐ monitors

☐ PC/base units

☐ keyboards

☐ mice

☐ telephones

☐ printers

☐ fax machines

☐ photocopiers

☐ scanners

☐ laptops

☐ mobiles

☐ pin machines.

This work is normally priced per clean, and the final cost depends on the quantity of items to be cleaned. You should have a pricing matrix for this type of service. Figure 2 is an approximate guide to the costs you could charge for cleaning the above items. You could use these costs as a guideline, but it is recommended you undertake some local market and competitor research to ensure your prices are in line. (*Note*: These prices may be subject to inflationary increases. It would be best to check these if you are unsure.)

A full PC (that is, a monitor, base unit, keyboard and mouse) should take about 15 minutes to clean, and an item such as a telephone only a few minutes. A quick multiplication of this time (based on the item prices in Figure 2 on page 25) will demonstrate the typical hourly rates you might generate from IT cleaning.

Cleaning IT equipment normally involves the following methods and materials:

☐ **Biological cleaning solutions**: available online or from local stockists.

☐ **Non-abrasive cloths and cleaning pads**: also available online or from local stockists.

☐ **Compressed air**: this comes in a canister.

☐ **Vacuum cleaning**: a special machine with a noise-reduction facility and suppressed sensitivity to electronic components and data.

An example of how you could present the cleaning process to a client is as follows. You would:

1. ensure that all the equipment to be cleaned is shut down or locked prior to cleaning to prevent accidental data loss;

2. brush clean all the keyboards (an anti-static foam cleaner would be applied, if required, and then vacuumed);

3. clean the keyboards and monitors with an anti-static cleaner;

4. clean the monitor screens with a lint-free cloth and anti-static screen cleaner and dry off with a microfibre cloth;

5. clean the mice and base units with an anti-static cleaner;

6. brush down the printers and clean them with an anti-static cleaner;

7. clean all the telephones with an anti-static cleaner;

8. undertake a visual count of all the items cleaned, to be agreed and signed off prior to invoicing; and

9. bag and remove all debris from the site.

This may seem like a highly technical process and one that you may feel unqualified to offer but, when you break it down, it is nothing more than a specific cleaning service for similar repeat items. It is advisable to undergo some training but, if you cannot, then some practice with your own or friends' and families' equipment will give you a good feel of the techniques required and of how the end result should look. There is, of course, the option to contract the work to a more experienced provider of this type of cleaning.

RELATED SPECIALIST CLEANS

There are a variety of similar add-on services with the same technical specifications as the above that you can offer to your clients. As with all the other services, do your homework and learn as much as you can from the Internet, from speaking to people in the industry, from reading up about the service and from training, where possible. These additional, related services include the following:

☐ **Server room cleaning**: IT industry research shows that up to 70% of computer-related breakdowns are caused by dust and other debris. The environment and the equipment itself are the source of this dust. This cleaning can be carried out in various types of computer room, from International Organization for Standardization (ISO) Class 2 clean rooms to general rooms used as server rooms. Because of the sensitivity of these rooms, unless otherwise required, they will be cleaned 'live' to reduce disruption to your client's business. A client meeting to discuss the clean levels to be achieved and the frequency of repeat cleans is advised.

☐ **Trading room cleans**: trading rooms contain a great deal of sensitive equipment, and the need to be online and up to the minute is a crucial part of this business. The general office cleaners will probably have been advised to steer clear of specific equipment to avoid problems, and this is why a 'specialist' clean is required in these areas. These cleans help to keep these areas sanitized and dust free and the equipment in the best possible condition.

☐ **Technical rooms**: again, the term 'technical rooms' can cover many things, but the things they have in common is that the general cleaning staff will have limited access to them and there will be various types of sensitive and expensive equipment that must be well maintained.

This is not an exhaustive list but the same principles and selling pitches apply to other, similar IT environments.

If you do introduce IT cleaning as one of your services, the best course of action is to train a member of your current staff – someone who has been with you for a while and who is reliable, intelligent and willing to try new things. You will have to pay them a higher hourly rate, but the return justifies this and it will ultimately save you having to spend the time doing the cleaning yourself.

Supplying cleaning consumables

Supplying cleaning consumables to clients may be regarded as more of a 'retail' than a 'service' function: you buy in cleaning products and then sell them on to clients with a mark-up on top. The reasons this function has been included here, however, are as follows:

☐ You will be buying cleaning materials and consumables for your own company anyway.

☐ Your clients will think you can supply these products because you use them yourself.

☐ There are good profit margins to be made.

☐ It is not a 'complaints' service in the way cleaning can be.

☐ The stock does not go out of date.

☐ Everyone needs such consumables as toilet paper, bin liners, etc.

If you want to have a real go at supplying materials and consumables, you will need storage space. This may not be feasible, however, if you have just started out because your storage space may be limited. You will need a decent-sized storage space because, if you are serious about supplying clients with cleaning materials, you should buy in bulk direct from the manufacturers. If you buy from a local supplier, what chance have you of winning local business when your clients can buy the same products from the same supplier without your mark-up on top? If you buy in bulk you will reduce your costs and will be both competitive and profitable.

Most manufacturers will require you to buy a full pallet of one particular item as a minimum purchase. This means a full pallet of toilet rolls, hand towels and so on. Your storage space will soon disappear because you will need to stock many different products. Take the time, however, to shop around for manufacturers and bulk suppliers – there are some who will offer mixed pallets, not to mention better prices.

If you do not have the storage space, you could buy from local suppliers as and when you need the items or when your clients order them. This is, of course, a much simpler way of managing things, but it will result in lower margins and slower growth. If supplying your clients is not a key area of growth for you at the moment, then perhaps this latter option is the better for the time being.

To begin with, concentrate on providing supplies to your current clients. For a typical office, you would probably supply the following repeat items:

☐ Normal toilet rolls and mini jumbo toilet rolls in different qualities and plies.

☐ Bin liners (swing, pedal and square).

☐ Black refuse sacks in different gauges.

☐ Centre-pull rolls (blue or white).

☐ Hand towels (different varieties and colours).

☐ A general selection of popular chemical products, such as hand soaps, washing-up liquids, dishwasher tablets, air fresheners and toilet-bowl cleaners.

☐ Mop heads and poles.

☐ Mop buckets.

☐ Cloths and dusters.

As your business develops you may want to add the following items to your stock list in order to attract a wider variety of clients and to offer a more comprehensive range of products:

☐ A full range of paper products in all varieties and colours.

☐ Brushes and brooms.

☐ Colour-coded cloths, scourers, gloves and general personal protective equipment (PPE).

☐ Floor maintenance equipment.

☐ A microfibre product range.

☐ Colour-coded mopping equipment.

☐ Tableware and glassware (potentially for sales and hire).

You may also want to supply a full range of chemical products, including the following:

☐ Auto-care and valeting products.

☐ Bar and cellar products.

☐ Biodegradable/environmentally friendly products.

☐ Hand cleaners.

☐ Disinfectants and bleaches.

☐ Floor-care products.

☐ Foil/film cleaners.

☐ General-purpose cleaners.

☐ A variety of trigger sprays.

☐ Machine-washing products.

☐ Oven cleaners and degreasers.

☐ Sanitizers.

☐ Hand soaps.

☐ Toilet cleaners.

☐ Detergents.

☐ Fresheners and deodorizers.

When deciding what prices to charge, you should check out what your competitors charge. This should not be difficult because you will more than likely have been buying from them while building up your core daily cleaning business.

You should keep your pricing simple. Set a margin that you apply to all the products you sell. For example, with a 30% margin across the board:

☐ A pack of toilet rolls costs you £5.00. Add a 30% margin. You sell for £6.50.

☐ A box of hand towels costs you £10.00. Add a 30% margin. You sell for £13.00.

This is one option, but you may choose a different margin for each product. You may even choose different margins for different clients. This is standard practice to benefit regular, high-spending clients. For example:

☐ X Ltd purchase 20 packs of toilet rolls per month. Their margin could be 25%.

☐ Y Ltd purchase 1 pack of toilet rolls per month. Their margin could be 40%.

There is no doubt that you should reward and encourage high-spending clients with both better offers and improved margins. On the other hand, you should also be looking to increase your margins to the highest possible levels. Do not, therefore, be shy to sell products at 100% or even 200% margins or more if you feel you can get away with it: it is not up to you to decide what is and is not a good deal. Let the customer decide this for themselves – your job is simply to be as profitable as you can while still appearing to be competitive.

If this side of your business is to grow, you will need to market your products and prices aggressively. You should offer a free delivery service, and most clients will require 30-day credit terms. It is at this stage that the nature of your business will change – it will become more of a retail enterprise and will require a retail management approach that is different from a service industry management approach. This may be a positive thing – you are building this side of your business and you may want to concentrate on this as your core business activity. Only you can decide this.

3

STARTING UP

Now that we have looked at the cleaning industry and the various services you can offer, it's time to consider your business's start-up requirements. Running any business, let alone a cleaning business, is demanding, and the service industry is a particularly hard industry because clients expect good service as standard. This chapter, therefore, aims to guide you through these first steps in setting up your business.

Becoming self-employed

There are many advantages in being self-employed, and these advantages will differ depending on the type of business person you are and the type of business you are running. You will measure your success differently from other people. Simply to be your own boss may be enough for you; for others, it may be the pursuit of wealth.

It is likely you are considering moving into self-employment for one of the following reasons. To:

☐ improve your income significantly;

☐ be your own boss;

☐ change your career path;

☐ improve your skills and knowledge;

☐ introduce a new product or service (a gap in the market); or

☐ take advantage of an opportunity.

It may be that a number of the above reasons are applicable to you, and no particular one represents the best reason why someone will become successfully self-employed. To have the best chance of being successful, you should do some homework on your chosen venture. Reading a book such as this is a good step to take: don't pour your cash into something you are unprepared for.

Consider carefully every step you must take because it is the culmination of these steps that will give you the best possible foundation to build on. Seek advice from your business gateway or from people you currently know who are running a cleaning business. When you have done this homework and have really thought it through, and when you have considered your finances and operating plans, you should be in a position to make an informed decision about whether you should commit yourself to becoming self-employed. If you are left with any doubts, take some more time and perhaps look at other options. Don't invest your money foolishly in something you are not prepared to commit yourself to.

If you are left with no doubts, you should be thinking the following:

☐ A cleaning business is what I want.

☐ I have the skills to run a cleaning business.

☐ I have the resources to start a cleaning business.

☐ I have the temperament and the attitude to make the business work.

☐ I know what is involved and what is required of me.

☐ I understand the responsibility I am taking on.

If your thinking is in line with the above, now ask yourself these final questions:

☐ **Will you enjoy running a cleaning business?** Remember, you are going to be spending a great deal of time doing this. If you don't think you will enjoy it, then perhaps this is not the business for you.

☐ **Are you prepared for the commitment?** If you give up on things easily or are easily frustrated, then self-employment may not be for you. You will be constantly challenged: you will need to find answers and not run away from problems.

☐ **Are you prepared for the risks involved?** Perhaps you are giving up your job to run a cleaning business. Do you understand that success is not a given and that there is a chance you could go out of business and potentially lose some or all of your investment?

☐ **Can you exercise patience?** Some small businesses will make no profits for the first couple of years. Growth will be slow while you learn and become familiar with your new industry. Have you got patience and faith that things will come good?

☐ **Are you flexible?** If you can't miss your Saturday golf round or your Thursday-night dance class, then you are not as flexible as you should be. You have to create a lifestyle that allows you to drop and run as your business requires.

☐ **Have you considered your family?** Do you have children, a mortgage or other financial commitments? Your income in the first couple of years will be, and should be, low so that you do not burden your business financially.

☐ **Are you in possession of the right skills?** Do you have a natural ability to cope in most situations? Can you show leadership as well as understanding? Can you clean floors and also keep financial records? Can you sell and market your services and also chase debt? Your skills should be adaptable.

☐ **Are you in a good state of health?** If you get depressed or stressed very easily, then self-employment is not a wise option for you. Both mental and physical health are required. Long working hours and the need to be hands on come as standard.

Remember, you are the key to your own success. Have faith every step of the way, think positively at all times and success will be yours. If you get your business model right, the sky really is the limit.

Naming your business

It may sound a little extreme, but choosing the right name really can make or break your business: if you have a vague name, clients will not understand what it is you are offering and will naturally contact a company that 'sounds' like it offers the services they require.

Try to avoid choosing silly or comedic names. This is bound to give the impression that you are unprofessional and are not entirely serious about your business intentions. Also take into account the following:

☐ **Avoid asking for too much advice from others.** While there is nothing wrong with a little informal consultation with friends or family, try to avoid including everyone in the process as everyone always thinks they know better! You can choose one name only, and it is guaranteed someone will be left with their nose out of joint. You could also end up in a compromise situation – a name no one really wanted and that will not be very good. Only ask those closest to you who you will offer some impartial thoughts and advice.

☐ **Take care with mish-mash names**. A popular and allegedly 'modern' method of choosing names these days is to mix adjectives and nouns – a mish-mash of words that may have the right intentions behind them but that end up looking silly. An example of this is to take the obvious verb 'clean' and a related verb such as 'dusting' to create 'Dustoclean'. This is just a little bit lame.

☐ **Avoid being too plain**. Aim for something slick and unique. Do not choose words that are normally associated with a certain company or group because this could be construed as plagiarism. Another 'buzz' word to avoid is 'solutions'. While this is a good tag to your main name, it is currently overused and is thus not unique.

☐ **Consider location names carefully**. Many companies choose a name based on their operating areas (e.g. Cambridge Joinery or Glasgow City Plumbing). While there is nothing wrong with this, it may hinder you as your business grows. Clients may assume you cover only your 'named' areas.

☐ **Avoid obvious clichés**. You will naturally be drawn towards positive, complimentary power words to enhance your base name: Ace Cleaning, Capital Cleaning, Alpha Cleaning, etc. While there is nothing at all wrong with these, they tend to be a little obvious and clichéd.

☐ **Obscure names are not advisable**. Potential clients should be able to work out what it is you offer as a company from your name. Your name can still be great without having to include 'cleaning', but avoid words that are hard to read and pronounce.

☐ **Consider the Internet and email**. Before settling on your chosen name, you will require a website and an email address. Check that you can get an appropriately matched domain name: it will appear odd if your company's name and the address of your website or email are completely different.

☐ **Check your local competitors**. You may have already chosen a great name, but is it exclusive? Make sure you do some market research to find out if anyone else has the same name. If you are setting up as a limited company, you can do a free directory check on the Companies House website (see Appendix I) to make sure no one else has the same name.

☐ **Be willing to change if need be**. The name may start fine but, as your company and services grow, it may become unsuitable or may limit your development. In the early years your brand will not be fully established, so don't be afraid to change the name if this is what you really want. Simply consider the costs in terms of stationery, etc.

Choosing your legal entity

What type of legal entity your business will have is an important first decision to make. This decision will be determined by a number of factors, such as going into business with a partner or, if you already have other business interests, how these will be affected by your new operations. The decision you make will have implications for how you report your accounts and for how you pay your taxes, when you pay them and how much you pay. There are four main legal entities, each of which has both its advantages and disadvantages in relation to tax and your legal obligations.

SOLE PROPRIETOR (OR SOLE TRADER)

A sole proprietor (sometimes known as a sole trader) is basically what the term itself suggests: a business owned and operated by a single person. As the sole proprietor and owner of the business, you will have responsibility for the debts and liabilities accrued by your business. You will also retain ownership of the business's assets. The profits you generate as a sole proprietor are combined with any other income you may have for income tax purposes.

The sole proprietor is generally regarded as the easiest of the four main entities to set up and operate because it does not need to constitute a specific legal form: as a sole proprietor you are not governed by any special rules or regulations.

PARTNERSHIP

A partnership comprises two or more individuals working together to run a business. Each partner has a specific role in the business and owns certain parts of the business and its assets. They also share responsibility for the company's liabilities. The allocation of ownership, responsibilities and liability should be set out in a partnership agreement because creditors have recourse to the personal assets of each of the recognized partners should they pursue debts owed by the partnership.

Partnerships are governed by certain laws. As a partner, you will have both rights and responsibilities under these laws. For example, you can borrow money and obtain credit but your creditors will request a personal guarantee. You are also required to file an income tax return. Again, your profits will be combined with any other personal income to determine your overall tax liability.

LIMITED COMPANY

A limited company is a legal entity that exists under authority granted by statute – in other words, a limited company can be regarded as a 'person' in its own right. It thus has its own legal rights and duties and it carries its own debts. It is also liable for the tax on the income it generates and it must therefore file a tax return. In most cases the company's owners or shareholders are protected from the liabilities the company has. In the early stages of your business, however, you might still be required to provide personal guarantees before being granted credit.

A limited company must adopt and file a 'memorandum and articles of association'. This governs the company's rights and its obligations to its shareholders, directors and officers. A limited company must also file a corporation tax return.

From an owner's point of view, the legal protection afforded by limited company status can be beneficial – you are not personally liable for the company's debts. Limited companies also have a number of other advantages, such as the ease of raising additional capital through the sale of share capital or by allowing individuals to sell or transfer their interests in the business. Limited company status also provides for business continuity: when the original owners retire they can choose to sell their shares, thus effectively selling the business on.

LIMITED LIABILITY PARTNERSHIP (LLP)

The limited liability partnership (LLP) is a relatively new form of business entity that became available for use in 2001. The LLP offers not only limited liability but also tax benefits and greater flexibility in its organization.

An LLP remains a separate legal entity from its owners/members. It is, therefore, responsible for its own liabilities and assets. This avoids the problems that can be experienced in a normal partnership whereby all the partners must be included in formal decisions and in signing legal or binding documents or agreements. What you gain in limited liability, however, you lose in terms of public information about your financial status. You are required to file audited accounts on an annual basis to Companies House, which include information that could potentially be considered private (such as profit share, etc.). The names and addresses of owners/members must also be filed.

The LLP itself is not taxed on its income or capital gains. Instead, the owners/members are taxed on their share of the LLP's profits and gains, just as partners in a partnership are currently taxed. The result of this is that, in certain circumstances, an LLP can be more tax efficient than a limited company: a limited company is taxed on its income and capital gains, and its shareholders are taxed on their financial return from the company, resulting in the undesirable situation of double taxation.

Working out the initial costs

Different types of businesses have different types of start-up costs. Unless you are buying expensive equipment that is essential to your start-up, you will find that a service business (such as cleaning services) does not require a heavy initial investment. Some capital outlay, of course, will be required so, at the very least, you should have access to a moderate investment fund.

To determine what costs you will require, you should identify and understand the expenses that will be incurred during the start-up period. These costs will be divided into one-off costs and ongoing costs.

You should expect the following costs as a minimum:

☐ **One-off**: a vehicle; initial equipment purchase; stationery, business cards, etc.; an accounting program (such as Sage or Quickbooks); uniforms; legal or professional fees (e.g. for incorporating your company if you choose to become a limited company).

☐ **On-going**: your salary; cleaners' wages (fortnightly); insurance; chemicals and materials; telephone costs; rent and utilities if you have an office; advertising.

There will also be additional costs to consider. You should decide which of these are essential and which are optional. The optional costs can be delayed until you have profit coming in. You could then use this profit for reinvestment.

You must be realistic from the outset and be aware of both your overheads and spending. Create a worksheet: put your numbers on paper so that you can add up all the costs and thus ascertain a realistic starting budget. There are also websites that offer start-up cost calculators. For example, the Alliance & Leicester has a start-up cost calculator that is industry specific and that includes contract cleaning (www.alliance-leicestercommercialbank.co.uk/bizguides).

You should also consider having a cushion fund on the off-chance you pick up fewer clients at the start than you anticipated. You may find that some clients pay late, so it is extremely helpful to have some funds available when things are tight.

The following are some further tips about setting up your business from the Small Business Success website (www.smallbusinesssuccess.biz).

LOCAL BUSINESS LINK

A good starting point is your local business link office (Business Connect in Wales, Scottish Enterprise and Invest Northern Ireland). Go to www.businesslink.gov.uk to find out where your local office is.

Book an appointment to see an adviser. This person will have a wide range of information and experience that will give you a good idea of the costs you will have to pay. This service is free.

CHAMBER OF COMMERCE OR LOCAL BUSINESS CLUB/GROUP

Local chambers of commerce or any other formal or informal business groups are a good source of knowledge and information. In these groups you will find a wealth of experience and people who have been through it all – both good times and bad! You may be lucky enough to attend a meeting where the speaker covers just the topic you are looking for.

COLLEAGUES AND OTHER BUSINESS OWNERS

If you don't have a club or group you can attend, then seek out business people yourself. Ask all your contacts to tell you about their start-up experiences: what costs they budgeted for, what costs they didn't budget for and where they overspent. Genuine business people are usually happy to share their experiences and to give you advice.

Should you have no business contacts, speak to your friends – some of them will have friends or relatives who are in business on their own. Ask for an introduction or referral. This will 'warm' them up before you meet them.

BANK BUSINESS GUIDES

Many banks produce brochures on starting up in business. These usually contain a business plan template that includes a section on start-up costs. Some produce guides for specific industries and sectors. These guides provide an in-depth analysis of the business, the market, the competition and the estimated start-up costs. You could also make an appointment to see your bank's small business manager/adviser.

SUPPLIERS

To cost your cleaning materials and equipment, phone your potential suppliers and ask them for quotations. Tell them you are starting up in the cleaning business and they should be more than helpful – after all, you could become one of their customers!

Deciding where to base yourself

The obvious initial choice is to base yourself at home. However, depending on what sort of a person you are, working from home could be beneficial or distracting – when you should be concentrating on work, your mind wanders elsewhere.

If you are going to be working from home, you will require the following:

☐ A computer.

☐ Internet access.

☐ A fax machine or a fax program.

☐ A printer (preferably combined with a copier and scanner).

☐ A dedicated area to work in (such as a spare room).

☐ Storage space for cleaning materials and chemicals, etc.

☐ A separate business telephone line.

When you work from home, you should try to apply yourself to 'work time' without too much 'home time' creeping in. In the early stages you may have some spare time, but you should use this to market and sell your business. Set yourself a start time, a lunch period and a finish time as you would have in a normal job, and try to stick to these times.

Working from home is the most cost-effective way to start your business, but you may feel from the outset that a commercial or city address would give your company a stronger image. While it would more than likely be financially unfeasible for you to lease a city-centre office, you do have the option of creating a virtual office.

The following are some of the advantages of using a virtual office:

☐ Professional telephone answering.

☐ An impressive meeting location.

☐ A 'big business' address.

☐ A mailbox service.

☐ Call forwarding.

☐ 24-hour voicemail.

☐ Fax facilities.

☐ Meeting rooms and short-term office space.

Virtual offices are widely available and start from as little as £25 per month. Contact your local business centres to find out their rates or contact a national business centre chain, such as Regus. Business centres also offer the added option of you being able to hire their facilities (such as training or meeting rooms) when your home won't quite give the right image.

Forget profit: chase success

Don't be alarmed by this statement. While the focus of any business is ultimately profit – pure and simple – if you forsake any of the key requirements of running your business just for an extra couple of pounds profit, then you will not last long.

Avoid silly things that will ultimately have a negative effect on your success. Don't, for example, buy the cheapest possible cleaning materials, don't argue with clients over a few pounds here or there, and don't pay the least amount possible to your staff or avoid investing in training, new equipment or essentials (such as uniforms for your cleaning staff). At the same time, don't overindulge: try to take a commonsense approach and think of the bigger picture. If you keep an eye on costs and focus on becoming the best and most successful at what you do, then the profits will follow.

What does the term 'an unsuccessful business' mean to you? The obvious answer is a business that has failed and that has made no money/profits. Now, what does the term 'a successful business' mean to you? Again, the obvious answer is a business that is making money. Consider, however, the following ten tips for success when starting up a new business from the Startups website (www.startups.co.uk):

1. Find a mentor – someone with the sense to see which way you are heading and who will help to steer your motivation in the direction of success. A partner can help, or consider using a life coach or business mentor.

2. Set yourself realistic targets. Break down longer-term goals into targets for this year, this month and this week. Have a checklist of things to do each day.

3. Think positively – congratulate yourself on all the things you have achieved rather than the few you haven't, and remind yourself that you have achieved something each day.

4. Visualize success – think in terms of what you want rather than in terms of the obstacles in your way.

5. Make time for family and friends. The chances are that the desire to provide for your family is motivating you anyway, so make sure that relationships are still strong when you achieve that success.

6. Recognize that breaks are beneficial and leave you remotivated and refreshed. Switch off the computer, get a good night's sleep and plan a holiday.

7. Look after your health – if that breaks down, so does your business success. Make time to eat well, to relax with your family and friends and to keep yourself fit.

8. If you work from home, separate your working time from your leisure time. An Abbey National survey revealed that 81% of males and 68% of females worked longer hours

since starting to work from home.

9. Identify what really motivates you – money, independence, a fresh challenge? If it is money, then concentrate on the projects that give you the greatest returns. Likewise for challenge or independence.

10. Take a step back. If a problem seems insurmountable, ask for advice from someone who works in a different industry. This should given you a different perspective on the problem.

Creating your brand

The brand you create for your cleaning company will be the first impression a potential client has of your company. You should therefore send a visual image to your target clients that reflects your company and what it offers. A good brand can be identified simply by sight (e.g. OCS and Initial in the cleaning world, and BT, McDonald's and Nike in the wider world).

Your company's first visual image will be your logo. This is something you should take some time to consider because it will stick with you. It is recommended you obtain some reasonably priced professional assistance with this as this will be money well spent. Homemade logos tend to look just that and ultimately send out the wrong image. Look at the two examples in Figure 3. Which do you think looks better? They are both in a single colour and are fairly basic, but the top one was made by a print-and-design company for next to nothing whereas the one below was made for free using Microsoft Word. The top has a little design and identity whereas the one below is just straightforward slanted text.

Fig. 3. Logos

When you have chosen your logo, try to put it everywhere you can:

☐ letterheads

☐ compliment slips

☐ general stationery

☐ business cards

☐ on company vehicles

☐ on your website

☐ uniforms

☐ in your email signature.

The more you display your logo, the more people will recognize it.

After your logo, the next brand identifier to consider is your company slogan. As a core message to potential clients, your slogan summarizes what your company stands for – for example, 'Committed to Clean!' Short, memorable slogans generally work better – certainly no more than two sentences. Ask for some feedback on your slogan to make sure it sends the same message to others as it sends to you.

Branding is, of course, more than just a nice-looking logo and a snazzy slogan. Branding is all about the thoughts and feelings you instigate in others when they see your brand and when they are on the lookout for a new cleaning company. Your branding should send out the message that you are the company they are looking for, and it should encourage them to phone you.

The following are 10 tips that may help you when working on your brand development.

1. THE DESIGN OF YOUR LOGO IS IMPORTANT BUT NOT CRITICAL

A nice logo will not guarantee success but it will help to identify what you offer as a company. For example, you would not choose a Mac computer rather than a Windows computer simply because you prefer the Apple logo.

2. DO YOUR BEST TO HAVE A QUALITY WEBSITE

When you visit a website, you can tell almost immediately whether it is professional or amateur. Every tool on your website a client may use should have at least a degree of professional quality. Use your website to emphasize your brand and to sell your services.

3. BLOGS ARE AN OPTION

If you want to have news and up-to-date content about your company online but the prospect of constantly updating your website seems onerous, you could consider blogs.

Blogs are extremely versatile things to use. You could have a link from your main website to your blog, and this could include images and news of recent jobs and achievements. It could also carry a list of up-to-date references from your clients.

4. GETTING YOUR BRAND OUT THERE

When the capital is available, consider a direct mail campaign or an email campaign. You could also host a webinar, sponsor a local event, attend a trade show, attend networking events, cold call prospects, win awards, etc. There are many ways to get your company noticed. What works for a cleaning company in London will possibly be different from what works for a cleaning company in Newcastle, so do your research to see what will work for you.

5. PREPARE A BROCHURE OR ONE-PAGE COMPANY OVERVIEW

It is good practice to leave something whenever you meet a potential client, whether this is a company brochure or a one-page company overview. Include all the relevant content, but don't overdo it!

6. INCREASE YOUR NETWORKING

Events are a great way to get your company brand in among industry people. Distribute your business cards wherever and to whomever you can.

7. KEEP YOUR BRAND PROMISES

It is very easy to talk about and to advertise a 'great service', but if you don't deliver that great service there will be little or no brand development. Unfulfilled promises and unmet expectations will lead to clients with negative views about your brand, and word soon spreads. On the other hand, if you meet expectations and keep your promises, positive words about your brand will travel.

8. OFFER A NICHE SERVICE

What will distinguish you from your competitors? Perhaps you will use only biodegradable cleaning chemicals. In this environmentally conscious age, people are drawn to this. You could also offer shorter contract terms or a free period of cleaning. Catch your clients' eyes so that they associate your brand with good business morals as well as with competitive pricing and flexibility.

9. ALL ACTIONS AFFECT YOUR BRAND

Everything you do – both seen and unseen – will have some effect on your brand. Whether it is marketing, advertising, vehicle choice, telephone manner or even stationery, you will find they all play their part in the development of your brand. Always consider what type of reaction each action will incur and how this will help (or hinder) your business and brand.

10. YOU ARE THE BEST ADVERT FOR YOUR BRAND

Meeting clients and being polite, professional and presentable are simple things that will help people associate your brand with quality. This also applies to how your employees behave.

Using the telephone

There is nothing worse than calling a business only to be answered by someone who simply says 'Hullo'. First, you will be unsure whether you have actually called a business at all and, secondly, you will be left feeling unimpressed and uninspired by the 'company' you were calling and potentially offering some business to. Think about what happens when clients call your business. How do you, or your staff, answer the phone?

- ☐ First is the greeting. When answering the phone, make sure you identify yourself and your company.

- ☐ Secondly, consider keeping a phone diary – a simple pencil and pad near the phone to jot down notes during conversations. This will help you to 'listen actively' and you will also have something to refer to later.

- ☐ Employ active listening noises, such as 'yes', 'I see' or 'great'. This lets the other person know that you care about what they have to say.

- ☐ Recap at the end of the call using your notes, and repeat any resolutions or commitments on either side to make sure you are both 'on the same page'.

- ☐ End the call on a positive note. Thank the other person for their time and express an interest in speaking with them again. If not, just let them know you appreciated speaking with them and end the call.

Almost everyone has a mobile phone these days. You could, therefore, provide a mobile phone number on your business card or even as a secondary contact number in an online or printed advertising directory, such as *Yell*. However, to have a mobile phone number as your main business contact number looks unprofessional and gives your clients the impression you are a 'one-man band' who probably does not have the resources to meet their needs.

When your company grows, consider purchasing a proper business telephone service. When your clients call, your phone will not ring: your clients will go instead to a welcoming automated message that will provide them with a few options. For example:

Thank you for calling The Cleaning Company. If you would like to speak to the office, press 1. If you would like to apply for a cleaning job, press 2. If you are a current client and would like to place an order, press 3. If you would like to leave a recorded message, press 4.

It is more than likely that, whatever option is chosen, the call will go to the same person, but that is not the point. The first impression will be that your company sounds extremely professional and perhaps larger than it actually is. The other facilities this service offers include a musically backed 'hold' facility, as well as voicemail and call transfer, etc. These are all small things that will help to create the right image for your company and that will promote your brand.

Telephone etiquette

INCOMING CALLS

When taking incoming calls, remember the following:

☐ All incoming calls should be answered in a timely manner. Always answer with a phrase such as: 'Good morning, The Cleaning Company, Robert speaking. May I help you?' The company's name should be stated as soon as the phone is answered, along with the name of the person who answered the phone. This lets the caller know they have reached the right business and lets them know with whom they are speaking.

☐ Avoid putting a caller on hold. If you have to, check back with them every minute or so and ask if they would like to continue to hold. This lets the caller know they have not been forgotten and that you are attending to their call.

☐ Speak clearly and slowly when you answer the telephone. Do not slur or mumble your words.

☐ Speak with confidence so that the person on the other end has the feeling you know what you are doing.

☐ Never be rude to a caller, no matter how nasty they are. Always handle yourself in a professional, business-like manner. This includes handling the situation in a calm, cool way.

OUTGOING CALLS

When making outgoing calls, remember the following:

☐ As above – speak clearly and slowly when you make a business call. Time may be money but, if the other party cannot understand what you are saying, you might as well have saved your breath and not made the call at all.

☐ When calling another business, it is proper etiquette to give your name and the name of the company you work for to whomever answers the phone. Do not make them guess who you are or make them pry this information out of you.

☐ If you get the wrong number, apologize to the person who answers the phone – do not just hang up. This is especially important now that people have caller ID on their phones: all they have to do is to check their device to find out who has just rudely hung up on them.

☐ When leaving a phone message, always state your name, company, phone number and reason for calling. Do not stammer or stutter, and do not use up an unreasonable amount of time.

Providing staff uniforms

Without wishing to be disrespectful, the cleaning industry suffers from a fair-sized element of poorly presented cleaning staff. All cleaning staff should have a uniform of some sort, depending on the type of shift they are doing – for example, for out-of-hours cleaning, a general cleaning tabard for women and a waistcoat for men and, for cleaning during office hours, dark trousers and shoes and a branded shirt or blouse.

In most instances, a tabard or waistcoat is acceptable, but you can provide primary-layer uniform items, such as T-shirts or polo shirts. While these may look good, from a financial point of view they will in fact cost you more because you will have to provide more than one garment per person for hygiene reasons. Purely from a cost-saving point of view and in light of the high staff turnover in the cleaning industry, a secondary-layer uniform (such as tabard or waistcoat) should suffice. These can be worn daily over primary clothing layers and, as long as they are laundered regularly, they will last for a long time.

As part of your brand identity you should consider having your company name and/or logo on your uniforms. Remember, however, that your full logo and an assortment of colours will be more expensive than your company name simply stitched on your uniforms in one colour. Stitched or embroidered uniforms always look better and last longer than screen-printed uniforms, so don't cut corners in this respect. Embroidered uniforms are not very expensive and the price comes down the more you buy.

It is easy to neglect your policy of having uniformed cleaning staff. You should, however, do your best to enforce it because nothing looks worse than a bunch of cleaning staff wearing tracksuits, jeans or whatever else in a professional business environment, particularly when clients are present.

4

KEEPING YOUR CLIENTS HAPPY

Your most unhappy clients are your greatest source of learning

(Bill Gates, founder of Microsoft)

This chapter looks at your potential clients. It should help you to understand them better because each client is different and will need to be treated differently. Bill Gates got it right – learning to read your clients is important. Not only will it help you to maintain relations and strengthen your position with your clients but it will also help you to develop your business and services.

Ensuring client satisfaction

The term 'client satisfaction' may be something of a cliché, but it is an inescapable fact that satisfying your clients is your main goal. Put simply, without clients you will have no business: staff can be replaced and profits can eventually be made or increased but, without clients, you have nothing. Above all, you must ensure your clients are happy with the service you provide. So what are the key things your clients will expect of you as a service provider? You will:

☐ be presentable and attentive in all you dealings;

☐ make time for them as and when they require you;

☐ listen to their concerns with both genuine interest and empathy;

☐ be proactive in dealing with requests, complaints and all correspondence;

☐ provide regular feedback or follow-up to them about anything you are working on; and

☐ be quick and responsive with quotes and information gathering.

Each of these points is discussed in detail below.

YOU WILL BE PRESENTABLE AND ATTENTIVE IN ALL YOUR DEALINGS

This point is really self-explanatory. The vast majority of your clients will not be impressed or encouraged if, for example, they call you for a meeting to discuss some complaints and you turn up with your tracksuit on, straight from the gym. Worse, you seem totally disinterested in their complaints. You should, of course, arrive punctually and dressed appropriately. While there is no need to go over the top with, perhaps, a full suit and tie, smart should be the minimum. Likewise, you should have a notebook and pen with you to take notes, and you should be prepared to absorb as much information as you can.

YOU WILL MAKE TIME FOR THEM AS AND WHEN THEY REQUIRE YOU

If you are all set for a lunchtime gym session and one of your clients calls to try to arrange an immediate meeting, what would you do? Tell them you can't make it and invent some excuse? Or realize how important it is to do what needs to be done – in other words, to 'do the right thing' from a business point of view? Inevitably the caller will be your worst client who is an incessant complainer about the smallest of things, but you must at all times put on your business head and deal with it appropriately. Never compromise in this: your business head must always come first if you are to succeed.

YOU WILL LISTEN TO THEIR CONCERNS WITH BOTH GENUINE INTEREST AND EMPATHY

Put yourself in your client's position. You are in a restaurant or trying to get through to your Internet service provider, for example. How frustrated would you be if you did not receive a decent level of service? Similarly, how happy and satisfied would you be if you were answered quickly and efficiently when you rang a large service provider like BT?

If your client complains that two bins were not emptied in an office of 400 people, deep down you might feel you want to tell them where to go. Your business head must prevail, however, and you must show deep concern at this 'tragic' happening and pull out all the stops to show interest and a willingness to resolve the problem at once.

YOU WILL BE PROACTIVE IN DEALING WITH REQUESTS, COMPLAINTS AND ALL CORRESPONDENCE

There is nothing a client hates more than having to repeat themselves to you or your cleaning staff, over and over again:

Monday: phone call – 'The window sills need dusting.'
Wednesday: phone call – 'The window sills did not get dusted.'
Friday: phone call – 'The window sills have still not been dusted.'

The following week
Tuesday: phone call – 'Window sills still not touched. I would like to have a meeting tomorrow.'
Wednesday: meeting – 'I am cancelling the cleaning as you are not providing the service I require.'

This can and will happen if you do not deal with complaints proactively. It is vital that a complaint is dealt with as soon as it is raised. You should, however, have noticed the problem before the client – something we return to later.

It is not just the complaints that should be dealt with proactively. If your client requires a copy of an invoice, for example, make sure they feel as though they are receiving a priority service. Deal with everything on a priority level, in fact, and you will not go far wrong.

YOU WILL PROVIDE REGULAR FEEDBACK OR FOLLOW-UP TO THEM ABOUT ANYTHING YOU ARE WORKING ON

Take the following example. The complaints have been coming in regularly and you feel the account is under threat of cancellation. You have informed the client you are going to replace the cleaning staff, change the hours of work, put together a new cleaning schedule and visit regularly to check standards. To the client this all sounds great, but telling them you are doing this is but one thing: all these recovery measures will take place when the client cannot see them happen. For all they know, after three of four days nothing has happened. The cleaning may be better but, for them at least, how long will this last? Tell them what you have done and keep them informed about measures that are still to be implemented.

YOU WILL BE QUICK AND RESPONSIVE WITH QUOTES AND INFORMATION GATHERING

To continue with the above example, you should visit, call or email the client every day to let them know about the progress you are making in resolving their problems – simply keeping them informed will help immeasurably in the client satisfaction stakes. If you are visiting or quoting for a new client, it will increase your chances several fold if you meet them or provide quotes as quickly as you can. In all situations, rapid and concise levels of feedback and follow-up will do no harm but good: when you sell your services to your clients and take on their business, you assume responsibility for everything. You must, therefore, meet all their expectations of a new service provider.

A very important point about client satisfaction is the retention of business. We will look at this in more detail in Chapter 7, but it is worthwhile considering it briefly here. Retaining your clients is vital if your business is to grow. In other words, your clients should not cancel your services. Offering excellent client satisfaction is one way of removing the 'reasons' for clients to cancel. Other ways include providing a good cleaning service and charging a competitive price.

Clients will cancel for any of these reasons, so don't think that, because your price is good, you can get away with poor cleaning standards or poor client satisfaction. All the 'boxes' must be ticked!

How clients regard cleaning

Unfortunately, everyone is an expert on cleaning: everyone has their own thoughts on what is clean and what is not clean. Not only this, but the office manager who complains to you about the cleaning is not the sole complainer. There will be an office full of 'experts' on cleaning who will complain to the office manager about the least little thing. So just as you are suffering from the burden of all these complaints, so is the office manager. Empathy in such a situation will not only help you to deal with the complaints but it will also help to strengthen your relationship with the office manager.

Cleaning is a necessity for most commercial premises but, from the client's perspective, it is an essential but resented financial overhead: cleaning is a cost that has no return. The office will be clean every day, but this is taken as given if the firm employs a cleaning company. In all your time running your business you will be able to count on one hand the clients who have called you to say: 'Thanks. Just wanted to let you know the office looked clean today. Great work!' This does not happen unfortunately. Your clients will expect the cleaning to be of a very high standard every single day. This is a demanding side of the business, not just physically but also mentally: one single day of a drop in service levels and the phone will be ringing with complaints!

Anticipating typical complaints

Because cleaning is regarded a cost burden by most clients, the service you provide (from price to standards and management) should be perfect. To stay one step ahead, it is as well to look at the typical complaints you can expect from your clients. While there seems to be a great deal of emphasis on complaints in this chapter, it is worth repeating that complaints are par for the course when running a cleaning business. Again, as Bill Gates so concisely puts it, complaints show you where you are going wrong and, provided you deal with them promptly and learn from them as you grow, they can be used constructively to help you improve your service.

Different types of cleaning services will generate different types of complaints. Using the services described in Chapter 2, the following should give you an idea of the types of complaints you may receive when providing these services. Whatever services you offer, it will pay to look at all these complaints now and to think about how you would prevent these problems from arising.

OFFICE CLEANING

Office cleaning is traditionally undertaken Monday to Friday. In most cases the cleaning happens 'out of hours' and the client rarely sees or meets the cleaner. These cleans average one to four hours per day, depending on the size of account and the number of staff provided.

Typical complaints include the following:

- ☐ The doors have been left unlocked.

- ☐ The alarm was not put on after the cleaning staff left.

- ☐ Items have been moved or have gone missing from people's desks.

- ☐ The crockery has not been cleaned appropriately.

- ☐ The bins have not been emptied.

- ☐ Vacuuming has been missed, particularly under tables.

- ☐ The dust levels are bad in such areas as skirting, sills, high levels and cabinets.

☐ The toilets have not been cleaned satisfactorily.

☐ The desktops have not been cleaned properly.

☐ The telephones have not been cleaned.

☐ Glass and pictures have not been cleaned.

☐ The cleaning staff are not working their full time.

☐ The cleaning staff are not coming in at their scheduled time.

☐ The cleaning staff are late or have not shown up.

☐ No supervisors have visited to check the cleaning.

PUB AND LEISURE CLEANS

Pub cleans are usually seven days a week cleans and are nearly always carried out under client supervision. There is, therefore, regular daily contact between the client and your staff. These cleans average two to three hours per day, depending on the size of the account and the number of cleaning staff provided.

Typical complaints include the following:

☐ The toilets have not been cleaned well enough.

☐ The toilets have not been restocked with toilet rolls, etc.

☐ The cleaning staff are arriving late.

☐ The cleaning staff are changing regularly (a consequence of weekend cleaning).

☐ The detail cleaning is not up to standard.

☐ The cleaning staff are leaving the shift early (five minutes early, ten minutes early).

☐ No supervisors have visited to check the cleaning.

BUILDERS' CLEANS

Builders' cleans are generally carried out over a short period of time – anything from one day upwards. These type of cleans usually last from four to seven hours per shift. The cleaning staff are normally the last workers in before the handover, and so there is often last-minute pressure to get the work completed on time.

With builders' cleans, a great many complaints arise when cleaned areas are made dirty again due to workers entering these cleaned areas. This 'repeat' cleaning should always be recorded because it is chargeable – it is not your fault or the fault of your cleaning staff. In almost all cases these cleans are supervised throughout by a member of the client's staff.

Typical complaints include the following:

☐ The carpets and floor coverings needed cleaning several times.

☐ Obscure areas of detail cleaning were missed.

☐ The staff had no personal protective equipment (PPE) on building sites.

☐ The staff were changed regularly, resulting in a lack of consistency.

☐ The windows or glass were not cleaned or needed repeat cleans.

☐ No one managed or supervised the cleaning staff.

☐ The cleaning staff did not arrive at a specific time or did not stay long enough.

DOMESTIC CLEANS

While domestic cleaning covers many areas, the following complaints mainly relate to one-off cleans, such as cleaning flats or houses for letting agencies or housing associations. These cleans are normally done in one day, and they usually come in at short notice. The average cleaning time will be anything from one hour to several hours, depending on the property's size and condition. In most cases, these cleans are not supervised by the client.

Typical complaints include the following:

☐ Under and behind couches have not been cleaned.

☐ Under and behind beds have not been cleaned.

☐ The ovens have not been cleaned to a 'sparkle'.

☐ The kitchen cupboards and drawers have not been cleaned in/out.

☐ The bathrooms have not been sufficiently detail cleaned.

☐ The 'smells' were not removed after the tenants moved out.

☐ The windows/glass have not been cleaned.

☐ Stains have not been removed.

☐ The rubbish has not been removed from the premises.

In addition, the new tenants will also possibly have complaints that will require an extra visit, which you will more than likely not be able to charge for.

WINDOW CLEANING

Window cleaning is normally undertaken by one person fortnightly, monthly or bi-monthly, either early in the morning or during working hours. Window cleaning is usually not supervised by the client but, when failings are noticed, this service is often scrutinized closely so that more apparent failings come to light.

Typical complaints include the following:

☐ Not turning up at scheduled times.

☐ The windows have been left streaky.

☐ All dirt has not been removed.

☐ The windows have been scratched.

☐ Dirty water has been left on the frames and sills.

☐ Items have been moved in order to get access but have not been returned.

☐ The window cleaner had a poor attitude or lacked manners.

☐ Proper health and safety procedures were not followed while working.

INDUSTRIAL CLEANS

The time required for industrial cleans generally depends on the size of the job, and most of this work is usually undertaken out of hours or at night (for example, for kitchen deep cleans). This type of work is often carried out without client supervision.

Typical complaints include the following:

☐ The results are not as expected (e.g. a client complains a kitchen has not been deep cleaned when all they asked for was a light clean).

☐ There were breaches of health and safety procedures.

☐ Other areas of the premises were damaged as a result of the cleaning (e.g. by dragging equipment or hoses across floors).

CARPET AND UPHOLSTERY CLEANING

This type of cleaning may either be planned for or required at short notice. As with industrial cleans, carpet cleaning is a skilled service, so clients are less likely to complain about carpet cleaning as they are about general cleaning. Cleaning times vary, and this type of cleaning may be undertaken both out of hours and during normal working times.

Typical complaints include the following:

☐ Stains or smells have not been removed completely.

☐ The machinery was too loud.

☐ The drying time was too long.

☐ The cleaners did not arrive at the arranged date or time.

CLEANING SUPPLIES AND CONSUMABLES

Complaints regarding cleaning supplies are usually less frequent than those associated with the other services you may provide. Deliveries are usually made during normal office hours.

Typical complaints include the following:

☐ Short deliveries or missing items.

☐ Wrongly delivered items or the wrong quantity.

☐ Poor-quality materials (e.g. cheap toilet rolls).

☐ The items were not delivered quickly enough.

☐ The items were not signed for, resulting in difficulties in receiving payment.

☐ The products did not perform to the expected standard.

IT AND SPECIALIST CLEANS

Because this is a specialist service, you will probably not provide a high volume of cleans in this area and will more than likely employ a contractor. Complaints, therefore, should not be a regular occurrence.

Typical complaints include the following:

☐ Due care and attention were not taken in the client's premises.

☐ Health and safety procedures were not followed.

☐ The results were not up to standard.

☐ Other areas of the premises were damaged as a result of the cleaning (e.g. by having to run cables or hoses across floors).

To summarize, therefore, if you bear in mind that a complaint is never far away, you will be on the alert to situations where problems could arise. It is, however, unlikely that you will ever achieve a completely complaints-free service, particularly as your company grows, but don't let the complaints put you off: look at the bigger picture.

Recognizing problems before they occur

You probably know the adage 'you get out of things what you put into them'. In other words, good results are only ever obtained through good efforts. Before you undertake a job, make sure you have considered the following:

☐ The job's requirements.

☐ The client's pet hates and annoyances.

☐ That you have put together a user-friendly and relevant cleaning schedule.

☐ Very importantly, that you have gone through all the above in detail with your staff and have trained them accordingly.

These few simple steps will ensure you have strong foundations from which to build your cleaning accounts. If you allow for problems and complaints in advance, you will not only avoid hassle but will also make sure you are seen as a professional and proactive manager – by both your clients and your staff. Word of mouth will result in potential clients approaching you, and these clients should be easy to take on.

In order to anticipate problems on an ongoing basis, you should perform some, if not all, of the following duties:

☐ **Visit clients regularly to obtain feedback on their thoughts on the service provided and to see if they have any areas of concern**. You may be surprised to find that some clients will have a long list of complaints they have not called you about. These situations warrant careful attention because clients who have lists of complaints but who have never contacted you regarding them are generally the clients who cancel completely out of the blue.

☐ **Obtain feedback from your cleaning staff to find out how they regard the work or if they are experiencing any problems**. Your main focus should, of course, be on the client, but this is a two-way street: your cleaning staff should also be given a forum to discuss any valid complaints or issues they have. In some cases there will be nothing you can do to resolve these issues because they will be minor, so you will, therefore, have to use your management skills to diffuse situations that do not warrant further action.

☐ **Undertake spot checks**. Spot checks on your cleaning staff should reveal any potential problems, particularly with out-of-hours accounts. If your staff have key access to premises, there may be a tendency for them not to work their complete shift. Instead of a two-hour cleaning shift as per your client agreement, a cleaner may arrive at 7 p.m. and leave at 8.10 p.m. – or even worse. Spot checks will ensure not only that the scheduled start times are being kept but also that the full cleaning time is being carried out: that cleaning work is actually happening, not staff sitting about chatting and drinking tea!

☐ **Perform audits on cleaning standards and follow these up regularly**. These audits can be done at any point during the cleaning shift or during your client's normal working hours. Simply arrange to visit or, if your relationship with your client is comfortable and informal, just drop in to suit yourself and inform the client you are there to carry out a standards check. The benefits of these audits are twofold: first, your client will see you being proactive in monitoring standards, which will have the knock-on effect of them not feeling the need to look for problems themselves; secondly, you will have an opportunity to find areas that may need improving and that perhaps have not as yet been noticed by the client.

Keeping your clients informed

As you will have no doubt noticed, clients can be a fickle bunch. You will work extremely hard to ensure they are satisfied with the service provided, and these background efforts will mostly go unnoticed and, moreover, unappreciated. This is a good reason to keep your clients informed: let them know what you are doing to provide them with a smooth-running service. Your clients do not need to know about everything that is going on, but you should definitely keep them informed about the following:

☐ **Meetings with your cleaning staff**. Tell them about any meetings you have had with your cleaning staff to discuss areas you feel need improving or to discuss changes in the frequency of certain aspects of the cleaning or any other changes of approach in the cleaning shift or cleaning schedule.

☐ **Audits on cleaning standards**. This is an opportunity for you to show the client that you have identified certain areas you plan to address with the cleaning staff and also to follow up on. It is a good idea to downplay your findings slightly. If you were shocked at the level of cleaning, there is no reason to let your client know this, particularly if they have not complained. It would be better simply to say that you have found a 'couple of areas needing a bit of attention'. There would be no harm in mentioning a few select areas, such as 'the microwave is needing a deeper clean' or 'I'm not too happy with the high dust levels'. This will show you are aware of areas of concern and that you are relaxed and confident in dealing with them.

☐ **Changes in cleaning staff**. There are several reasons why it is important to notify your client about changes in cleaning staff, and the first and most obvious concerns security. Clients do not want a different member of cleaning staff every other night or every other week. They want consistency because this will give them peace of mind from a security point of view. Similarly, clients come to know the cleaning staff – they might see and speak to them every night or morning. If cleaning staff suddenly disappear and strange new faces appear, this can be disconcerting for the client.

☐ **Problems with cleaning shifts**. Any number of problems can happen during a cleaning shift – anything from staff sickness or fainting, to staff getting locked behind doors, to alarms going off. You will never fail to be surprised by some of the things that can happen when working with cleaning staff! Due diligence should be followed and a brief, downplayed report sent to the client at the earliest possible opportunity.

☐ **Access problems**. Access problems are a regular occurrence with out-of-hours cleaning. Keys will be lost or snapped in doors. Key fobs will not work or will not have been programmed properly. Alarm codes and procedures will be wrong or will not be followed correctly. All this will result in phone calls to you very early in the morning or very late at night and, again, on resolving such problems, you should inform the client about the occurrence and the outcome at the earliest opportunity.

☐ **Extra cleaning**. Keep your client informed about any extra cleaning you have undertaken if for no other reason than to show yourself in a good light. If you carried out a deep clean or an extra bit of detail cleaning free of charge, you should make sure your client is aware of how charitable you have been in providing this additional, free cleaning!

Remember, the whole point of keeping your clients informed is to show both you and your company in a good light. This is a showcase of your management ability: it is a demonstration of the effort and application you are providing to your clients to give them your best possible level of service.

5

MANAGING YOUR STAFF

(Catherine the Great, Empress of Russia)

The above quotation sums up neatly how you should manage your staff. Learning to manage your staff, however, will be one of the greatest challenges in running and growing your cleaning business. While most businesses generally have few part-time staff, cleaning businesses will have a great many, and with lots of staff come lots of problems and challenges. Moreover, staff can both harm and benefit your business. This chapter, therefore, looks at the various issues related to managing your staff.

Employing staff

The simple fact is, your staff will make your business: your staff and how they conduct themselves will be a reflection of your business. When your staff act inappropriately, or when they are ill-mannered or badly presented, this, in your client's eyes, represents your company and the service you provide. In most cases clients simply associate bad staff with a bad company. This must be avoided at all costs. While sometimes a bad apple will get through, once identified it must be deal with accordingly. Cleaning staff tend to be a mixed bunch of both the good and bad. When you find good staff, you should do all you can to keep them because good staff can be few and far between.

Motivating and rewarding staff

It is widely accepted that recognition is an extremely important management tool when dealing with staff: a simple 'Thank you' may be all that is required. Recognition is vital for motivating staff. If a member of your staff is always reliable, well presented and hard-working, then you must tell them from time to time what a help this is to you and let them know how grateful you are for their diligence. This will definitely lift their spirits and will show them they are appreciated.

The following are some tips on motivating staff:

☐ **Involve your staff in the decision-making process**. People are inclined to work harder if they know their ideas are appreciated and acted upon.

☐ **Listen to your staff**. Do not dismiss staff grievances or complaints. Provide a forum where points and issues can be raised.

☐ **Communicate clearly**. If your staff do not understand what it is you are asking them to do, it is unlikely you will get a positive reaction. Communicate clearly and they will understand and react positively.

☐ **Do not over-control**. Communication is a two-way process. If you do not listen to your staff, they will resent this and this will be reflected in their work.

☐ **Recognize your staff's achievements**. As mentioned above, a simple, regular 'Thank you' or 'Good job' will be appreciated.

☐ **Reward when appropriate**. You are running a business so expensive gifts are a no-no, but a bottle of wine or bunch of flowers every now and again will do nothing but good.

☐ **Appraise your staff**. Appraisals are an opportunity for you to sit down and go through formally the positives and negatives about your staff's performance.

☐ **Be tactful**. If there is a need to supply some constructive criticism, be tactful. Adopt the 'smack it and rub it better' technique – in other words, follow a negative with a positive.

☐ **Stick to your word**. If you have promised a certain day off or a wage increase, you must stick to your word. If you do not deliver what you say, your staff will lose faith in you.

☐ **Create a team**. Your staff must feel as though they are part of a team. All contributions should be recognized in some way so that everyone feels included.

Finding staff

Most new cleaning accounts will not start immediately, so you will have the time to advertise to find new staff. Occasionally, however, a client will ask you to start at short notice and, if you are unable to say yes, they will simply find another company that can. In such circumstances you are advised to say yes, whether you have the staff or not. This will put you under pressure to obtain new staff or to get cover staff in place, but you should try not to lose the new account. If the worst comes to the worst, you may need to carry out the cleaning yourself, but such a situation will give you the incentive to find some new staff quickly. It is worth noting here, however, that no matter how urgently you need stuff, you should avoid employing a 'family' team (two sisters or a mother and son, for example). If there is a family emergency, both may not show, perhaps leaving you with not staff at all!

You should put together a simple database to record the people who have contacted you for a job. While you may not require any additional staff when someone applies, make a record of their details because it is people like these whom you'll call when a new account starts or other staff leave. There is no time limit for how long you should hold this information: just because you have held someone's details for three months or even three years does not mean you cannot call them when the time is right. A simple database such as the one shown in Figure 4 should suffice. This could be handwritten or kept on your computer using Microsoft Word.

Name	Date applied	Home number	Mobile number	Location	Notes
Ian Baker	August 2008	01234 567 890	07899 123456	Manchester central	Career cleaner
Jane Glynn	March 2008	07788 998 877	01723 456789	Sallford	Can use buffer

Fig 4. Cleaning staff database

Apart from recording their full name, make a note of when they first applied and try to obtain both their home and mobile phone numbers. Home phone numbers change less frequently than mobile numbers. 'Location' is an important section. Should you have a new account starting in Salford, it would make more sense to contact Jane Glynn than Ian Baker. In the last column, note the experience, skills or any opinions you may have of the person who called.

When you decide to contact a potential employee, a short phone call such as the following is the next step:

Hi, is that Jane Glynn? This is Robert from The Cleaning Company. You called me back in March looking for a cleaning job. I had nothing for you at that time, unfortunately, but I recorded your details as you sounded to me like a good potential employee I wanted to call when something appropriate came up. Are you looking for a job just now? Do you still live in Salford? That's great. Here are the details of the job . . .'

Something informal such as the above will give a good impression: you thought the person sufficiently suitable that you went to the trouble of keeping their details and coming back to them months later. In fact, the situation suits you perfectly because Jane Glynn lives a short bus ride from the new account and is interested in the position you have available.

Sometimes, however, there will be no one on your database who is suitable for the position you wish to fill, in which case you will have to advertise for staff. The following are some ways you can do this.

JOB CENTRES

Your local job centre is the obvious first choice: it will cost you nothing and it is relatively straightforward to use. You simply register with the job centre and they will provide you with an employer's reference number. Following this, you call a national contact centre where you provide details of the job you wish to advertise:

□ **Whether the position is temporary or permanent**. You should advertise your cleaning positions as permanent unless they are clearly temporary.

□ **The number of hours' work per week**. Multiply the number of hours per shift by the number of shifts per week.

□ **The number of days' work per week**. Make sure you mention whether weekends are involved or whether the days are to be 'five over seven', for example.

□ **The shift's starting and finishing times**. This is important information that a potential applicant will require.

□ **The postcode of the work's location**. This is the cleaning account's postcode, not your own. Knowing the postcode ensures the advertisement is run in the most appropriate location.

□ **The hourly rate or salary**. If possible, displayed this as 'starting at £X per hour'. This shows that the hourly rate may be increased.

□ **How long you want the position to be advertised**. Generally, it is best to advertise the position for as long as you can. If the position is filled quickly, any other people who apply can be added to your database.

□ **General description of the position and its requirements**. This is where you specify the type of work and applicant required. Emphasize key phrases, such as 'must be reliable' and 'experience preferred but not essential'. Provide a brief summary of what is involved in the cleaning shift.

□ **How you would like staff to apply for the position** (i.e. by application form or telephone call). For speed, ask that applicants contact you directly via the telephone so that you can take their details and organize interviews. In doing this, your contact details will be displayed on the Job Centre Plus website as well as provided to applicants who visit the local job centre.

Job centre advertising, however, is not always successful: your job may be overlooked among many others and, all too often, the response may be low.

LOCAL ADVERTISING

Advertising in the area where your new account is located is perhaps the best way to find new staff – very few cleaning staff will drive to their cleaning shifts and fewer still will travel long distances on public transport for what, more than likely, will be a short cleaning shift.

Local shops and post offices have noticeboards or card boards for adverts, as do some supermarkets. You should target all these. In most of these places you can advertise for free, and the ones that do charge are normally quite cheap – about one or two pounds for a couple of weeks' or a month's advertising. You should receive a good response if you advertise this way, the only difficulty perhaps being finding shops and post offices in areas you are not familiar with.

Your advertising card will probably be handwritten and may look something like Figure 5. Make sure it is general and informal – just the basics to garner some interest and to persuade potential staff to phone you. When they do phone, ask them where they saw the advert. This

> ## Cleaning Staff Required
>
> Local area – immediate start
> Monday to Friday – evenings
> £5.75 per hour starting rate
> Must be reliable and hard working
> Other positions also available
>
> Contact Robert for more details on:
> 01234 567 890

Fig. 5. Advertising card

will help you to assess the best locations to place adverts in the future, and you may have placed adverts for different jobs in different locations.

WORD OF MOUTH

Very often, cleaning staff know other cleaning staff, and the people who live in an area where you have recently taken on a new account may know someone who knows someone else who cleans. You will be surprised how successful word-of-mouth recruitment can be and, of course, it is free.

Using the same example given earlier in this chapter, Jane Glynn is doing a good job and word has spread: a potential client therefore contacts you looking for a quote. Jane is unable to take on these extra hours but she knows someone who can. Trust her word – you should find that really good staff only recommend people whom they consider to be of a good standard.

LOCAL NEWSPAPER AND INTERNET ADVERTISING

Should all the above fail, you could consider advertising in local newspapers and on the Internet. Most newspapers run a jobs available section that includes small classified adverts. While there will be a fee to pay to advertise in a newspaper, your advert should be seen by a large number of people.

There are various websites where job adverts can be placed. Some of these are expensive whereas others are free. The best thing to do, therefore, is to surf the Internet to find out what types of classified and community-based websites are most appropriate for your needs.

Conducting interviews

You do not need to conduct formal interviews – short meetings in which you can meet and assess the applicant and talk about the expectations you have of the staff who work for you should be sufficient in most cases.

While interviews cannot guarantee that the staff you eventually select will be everything you wanted, they will certainly help towards this end. During an interview you should aim to establish or to find out the following:

☐ The applicant's character, demeanour, background, skills and experience.

☐ How interested the applicant is in the position.

☐ The expectations you have of the person who will be appointed.

☐ Whether the applicant can work as part of a larger team.

☐ Whether the applicant is sure the job is right for them after finding out what the job entails.

☐ The applicant's presentation and general cleanliness.

You should also point out what is not acceptable:

☐ Arriving late.

☐ Short-notice absences.

☐ Absences without notice.

☐ Using client equipment or telephones.

☐ Theft.

☐ Bad presentation (e.g. turning up for work drunk or with a hangover).

☐ Tea or cigarette breaks.

While the intention should be to keep things light and informal, there are certain questions you should ask in order to obtain some key information:

☐ **Are you working at the moment?** If they are currently working, you should ask them why they have applied for your job.

☐ **Why are you leaving this job?** This could be for any number of reasons, but this question should help you to pick up some information that will influence your final decision.

☐ (If currently unemployed) **Why did you leave your last job?** For reasons similar to above. Also, if they have been unemployed for some time, you will want to know why.

☐ **How long have you been doing cleaning work?** This question will provide vital, experience-related information and will lead on to other important questions and answers (such as previous employers, tasks and achievements).

☐ **Do you have any problems with the hours and/or days of work?** There are people who apply for jobs that involve working on Monday to Friday evenings, for example, who, when asked this question, say: 'Oh, I can't actually work Wednesday nights.' It is best to find this out now.

☐ **Do you know what the hourly rate is?** The applicant should be aware not only of the hourly rate but also of the frequency of pay and of any other information that could potentially cause them to leave shortly after starting.

If someone does not have much experience of cleaning but otherwise seems suitable, do not rule them out. Cleaning is not difficult, and it would be a shame to reject someone because they were not a 'career' cleaner. Given time and training, this person could become one of your most valuable members of staff. Remember, reliability and consistency are every bit as important as cleaning skills and experience.

While during an interview you will be assessing the applicants' suitability, bear in mind that the applicants will also be assessing you as an employer. If you coming across badly during an interview, you may put off potentially good staff. You should thus sell yourself as an employer: be informal and share a joke but maintain an air of authority. This is not a difficult thing to do, and you will find that the more interviews you carry out, the more you will master these techniques.

Choosing the right place for an interview

Where you hold your interviews will depend on the vacancy you wish to fill. It will also depend on how many interviews you will be holding. The following are suggestions for places where you could conduct interviews.

AT THE PREMISES THE APPLICANT WILL BE WORKING IN

If you hold your interviews at the premises the applicant will be working in, this will demonstrate that the person can find the place of work should you offer them the job. It will also reflect well on you. It will show your new client that you are being conscientious in the selection of staff for their premises and will thus make you look professional. It will also make you look professional and businesslike to the applicant.

You should, of course, check that the client is happy for you to interview at their premises. For smaller cleaning accounts, this may not be suitable because space will be limited and the client may not see it as necessary to provide you with a room to carry out interviews. It may, however, be suitable for larger accounts where three of four staff will be working together, and larger accounts are unlikely to charge you for using their facilities.

PUBLIC MEETING PLACES

While your business is small and growing, you will most probably still be working from home and may be uncomfortable with the thought of interviewing people there. If this is the case, consider holding your interviews in a public place, such as a coffee shop, café or restaurant. Starbucks and Brewers Fayre are ideal meeting places and can come across as both informal and professional.

YOUR OFFICE OR HOME

Holding interviews in your own home may seem a little personal, and it is important that, as an employer, you put a clear line in the sand that you are a professional person with a position of authority. This line, however, may become blurred if you interview at home. Furthermore, if your staff have grievances or complaints in the future, you do not want them turning up at your home with them.

ON THE JOB

If the position is for a cleaning account you have had for some time, you could carry out a practical, onsite interview-come-trial. While this type of interview has it problems, it does help you to achieve the following:

☐ You see the applicant cleaning.

☐ The cleaning shift is covered.

☐ The applicant sees first hand what is involved in the job.

☐ The applicant learns the location of the premises.

This method of interviewing, however, means that you can only interview one or two applicants at a time. Also, if no one turns up, you will not only have wasted time preparing but you will also have to carry out the cleaning yourself! Similarly, you may have to consider paying the applicant for the cleaning they have carried out – if all goes well, this shift could count as their first.

THE APPLICANT'S HOME

This option is not recommended. It has been suggested that, by interviewing potential cleaning staff in their own homes, you will obtain a good impression of their standards by how their homes are presented. This method of interviewing could, however, be seen as an invasion of privacy, and it would probably make the applicant feel uncomfortable.

Training

You should not overlook training your cleaning staff. Proper training not only leads to cleaner buildings and happier clients but it also means fewer accidents, more productive cleaning times and a more professional image for your cleaning staff. Training involves both the work your staff undertake and the equipment and, in particular, the chemicals they use on a daily basis. Depending on the level and type of training you intend to undertake, a range of options is available, and this training can be carried out either in-house or by a professional training organization, such as the British Institute of Cleaning Sciences (BICSc).

While training conducted by an organization such as BICSc will incur a fee, there is a selection of courses to choose from and such organizations have training centres throughout the country. One of the most popular courses is the BICSc Cleaning Operators' Proficiency Certificate. (The tasks covered by this course are listed in Appendix II.) If you join the BICSc Cleaning Operators' Proficiency Certificate Scheme, you can become trained and appointed as an assessor. Alternatively, you could nominate someone else in your company for this role. BICSc employs an independent moderator who ensures the scheme is operated fairly and to a proper standard.

It is up to you to select the cleaning staff to be entered for the certificate. To qualify for a certificate, an operator must complete successfully the assessments for a certain number of skills:

☐ Stage 1: a minimum of ten skills.

☐ Stage 2: any ten of the remaining skills.

☐ Stage 3: any ten of the remaining skills.

The tasks to be assessed are entirely your own decision, and the assessments are carried out either by you or by your nominated in-house assessor. When the cleaning staff have successfully completed all the required assessments, BICSc is notified and certificates are issued. At the same time, you will receive an official record from BICSc of the personnel who have qualified for the certificate.

Proper training is essential if your employees are to work properly, safely and efficiently. The following tips should help to ensure your employees learn to do their jobs safely and efficiently:

☐ Cleaning workers rank highly in the most injured workers lists. Training your employees properly will not only keep them working but will also avoid expensive insurance claims.

☐ Keep the training focused on your employees and their needs. If training just one or two employees, use eye contact, ask questions and get them involved – don't just give them a lecture.

☐ Don't simply demonstrate products. Many cleaning staff only receive training when a new product or piece of equipment is introduced. Train your employees from start to finish.

☐ Make sure your training is effective. Demonstrate products and techniques and encourage your employees to become involved and to ask questions if they don't understand something.

☐ Use the Tell–Show–Do–Review technique. *Tell* (about each step), *show* (how to perform each step), *do* (each step) and *review* (each step).

☐ Measure the effectiveness of your training. It's difficult to know if your training time was well spent if you do not have some sort of measurement tool. This may be faster cleaning times, lower accident rates or the reduced use of cleaning products and supplies.

☐ Training can be boring. Don't just give your employees training manuals or product literature and expect them to read it and then have improved job performance. Find ways to make training interesting. Demonstrate new products and supplies instead of having your employees read about them. Give practical examples of how to be more efficient. Use your knowledge and experience and pass these on to your employees.

☐ Remember, you can learn from your employees. If they have picked up a technique that saves times or money or that makes the job easier, ask them to share it with the rest of your cleaning staff.

☐ Change is not always easy. Training involves changing behaviours and attitudes. The training may involve a new product or piece of equipment, or it may be to break bad habits. Either way, employees may be resistant to change. Don't be surprised when your employees are reluctant to change. Be prepared for this resistance and overcome it with information and statistics about why the change is needed.

☐ Proper staff training is essential – not just to make sure the job is done correctly and efficiently but also to keep your cleaning staff safe on the job. Keep your employees interested during training sessions by making the training hands on and informative.

Dealing with staff turnover

As noted elsewhere in this book, the cleaning industry has always suffered from a high staff turnover. It can, therefore, be quite demoralizing to spend time training your staff only for them to leave suddenly and to have to repeat the process all over again. The reasons for this high staff turnover are as follows:

☐ Cleaning jobs can be picked up fairly easy, especially in towns and cities.

☐ Cleaning jobs are generally low paid, although the national minimum wage has changed this to some extent.

☐ The work can be dirty and unattractive, particularly when toilet cleaning is involved.

☐ Some staff may only be looking for additional income for a short period of time to pay for holidays or Christmas, for example.

☐ Transport may be a problem, depending on the area where you require cleaning staff.

☐ The work is not particularly rewarding.

The obvious answer is to pay your staff more and, while this will certainly help, it is not the whole solution to staff retention. The problem is that cleaning is a competitive market, and clients will not be prepared to pay over the odds for a cleaning service just so that you can pay your staff more. The solution is to invest time and effort in your staff, which includes better hourly rates, recognition and rewards, as well as training and development.

London-based Blue Diamond Services has a turnover of £35 million. Harvey Alexander, the firm's chief executive, has said the following about staff retention: 'that is what our business is about, really – staff. If the workers do a great job, Blue Diamond is doing a great job – which in turn leads to more contracts. So we want to keep our employees.' To attract good workers in the first place, Blue Diamond pays 20% above the going rate, as well as providing comprehensive training, a guarantee of employment and a smart uniform. 'In addition, we've worked hard on developing our corporate brand,' says Alexander. 'We want people to be proud of working for Blue Diamond and wearing its name on their sleeve.'

Your responsibilities as an employer

As an employer, you will have responsibilities towards your staff. Most of these responsibilities are legal ones, such as employment law and health and safety, but you will also have a responsibility to treat your staff correctly from the outset. From a legal point of view, you must be extremely careful about your conduct as an employer. The Health and Safety Executive state the following:

☐ It is an employer's duty to protect the health, safety and welfare of their employees, and other people who might be affected by their business. As an employer you must do whatever is reasonably practicable to achieve this.

☐ This means making sure that your employees and others are protected from anything that may cause harm, effectively controlling any risks to injury or health that could arise in the workplace.

☐ As an employer you have duties under health and safety law to assess risks in the workplace. Risk assessments should be carried out that address all risks that might cause harm in your workplace.

☐ You must give employees information about the risks in your workplace and how you are protected and instruct and train them on how to deal with the risks.

Health and safety legislation cannot be compromised. You must always be aware of this and be seen to be complicit in every aspect of the legislation. You are legally bound to consult your employees for any of the following reasons:

☐ Changes that may substantially affect your employees' health and safety at work, in procedures, equipment or ways of working.

☐ The likely risks and dangers arising from your employees' work, measures to reduce or get rid of these risks and what they should do if you have to deal with a risk or danger.

☐ The planning of health and safety.

☐ The health and safety consequences of introducing new chemicals or technology.

In general, your duties will include the following. To:

☐ make the workplace safe and without risks to health;

☐ ensure plant and machinery are safe and that safe systems of work are set and followed;

☐ ensure articles and substances are moved, stored and used safely;

☐ provide adequate welfare facilities; and

☐ give the information, instruction, training and supervision necessary for your staff's health and safety.

In particular, you must do the following:

☐ Assess risks to your employees' health and safety.

☐ Make arrangements for implementing health and safety measures identified in risk assessments.

☐ If you have five or more employees, record the significant findings of risk assessments and the arrangements for health and safety measures.

☐ If you have five or more employees, draw up a health and safety policy statement, including the health and safety organization and arrangements in force.

☐ Appoint someone competent to assist with health and safety responsibilities and to consult your employees about this appointment.

☐ Co-operate on health and safety with other employers sharing the same workplace and set up emergency procedures.

☐ Provide adequate first-aid facilities and make sure that the workplace satisfies health, safety and welfare requirements (e.g. for ventilation, temperature, lighting, and sanitary, washing and rest facilities).

☐ Make sure that work equipment is suitable for its intended use so far as health and safety is concerned, and that it is properly maintained and used.

☐ Prevent or adequately control exposure to substances that may damage your employees' health.

☐ Take precautions against danger from flammable or explosive hazards, electrical equipment, noise and radiation.

☐ Avoid hazardous manual handling operations and, where they cannot be avoided, reduce the risk of injury.

□ Provide health surveillance as appropriate.

□ Provide for free any protective clothing or equipment where risks are not adequately controlled by other means.

□ Ensure that appropriate safety signs are provided and maintained.

□ Report certain injuries, diseases and dangerous occurrences to the appropriate health and safety enforcing authority.

Your staff's responsibilities

Your employees will also have legal responsibilities towards you: To:

□ take reasonable care of their own health and safety and that of others who may be affected by what they do or do not do;

□ co-operate with you on health and safety;

□ use work items provided by you correctly, including personal protective equipment (PPE), in accordance with training or instructions; and

□ not interfere with or misuse anything provided for their health, safety or welfare.

6

ORGANIZING YOUR FIRST CLEANING ACCOUNT

If you work just for money, you'll never make it, but if you love what you're doing and you always put the client first, success will be yours

(Ray Kroc, founder of McDonald's)

This chapter looks at your first meeting with a potential client and the stages that follow from this meeting.

Visiting your potential client

When you have made contact with a potential client, you should allow them to dictate the day and time of the meeting. This shows that you are flexible – you are able to see your client at a time suitable to them. From the outset you should be seen as amiable, professional and totally accommodating.

The following are a few things to consider before the meeting:

- ☐ The meeting's start time. Try to arrive at least five minutes early. This will give you time to compose yourself and to take in the surroundings.

- ☐ The company's full name and address and how to address your contact correctly. People can be offended if you get their names or the positions they hold in a company wrong.

- ☐ Your personal preparation. First impressions are all: if you are unshaven, hung over or wearing jeans and trainers, you will not do well. Make sure you look professional and that you come across as enthusiastic, friendly and confident. Confidence is important. Your general appearance should demonstrate to the client that you are the person to solve their cleaning problems.

It is a good idea to take with you a small presentation folder so that you can outline your services in a professional way. This folder should contain the following:

- ☐ A copy of your public and employers' liability insurance.

- ☐ An example cleaning schedule.

- ☐ Brief health and safety, equal opportunities and/or environmental policies.

- ☐ A generic risk assessment and methods statement.

☐ A priority contact list (telephone, fax and mobile numbers, etc.). This will demonstrate to the client that they will be able to contact you easily, should the need arise.

☐ Any awards or certificates that may support you in your bid for their business.

Most potential clients will already employ a cleaning company that they want to replace. If this is the case, you should try to establish the following:

☐ How many cleaning staff currently service their premises.

☐ Whether they work mornings or evenings.

☐ The cleaning times and days (e.g. Monday to Friday or weekends).

This information will help you to put your quote together. You should also ascertain the following:

☐ The access arrangements.

☐ Whether the current cleaning company provides consumables (toilet rolls, bin liners, etc.).

☐ Whether the client would prefer to receive your quote by post or email.

☐ The contract's start date.

☐ Any problems the client is experiencing with the current cleaning arrangements.

All the above should give you enough information to put together and submit a quote.

The client will next show you round their premises. Use this tour to point out areas of the client's current cleaning service that you are not impressed with. Some areas where you may catch out the cleaning staff are as follows:

☐ The fridge (especially the shelves).

☐ The cutlery drawer.

☐ The legs of seats and desks (check for dust).

☐ The underside of the sinks in the toilets.

☐ The underside of toilet bowls and around the seat hinges.

☐ The bins (for stains) – especially kitchen bins.

☐ Tiled splashbacks.

☐ General dust levels.

Don't be afraid to point anything out that should be attended to, and tell the client you will resolve these issues as soon as you take over the account.

Making and submitting your quote

Do your best to send your quote to the client on the same day as the meeting. This will not only emphasize your efficiency but you may also be awarded the contract before your competitor even submits their quote.

WORKING OUT YOUR QUOTE

To work out how to put your quote together, we'll use the following example. Z Ltd require two cleaning staff for two hours per evening, five days a week. First, you should establish a rate for your cleaning service. This rate will depend on many factors, from the size of the job, to its location, to the cleaning time. Also bear in mind the adage: 'the more you buy, the less it costs.' In other words, if you have a client who requires eight cleaning staff a day for four hours per cleaning shift, they will expect a lower rate than a client who requires one cleaner for one day a week for two hours.

As a general rule, base your quote somewhere between £8 and £10 per hour. In the case of Z Ltd, £9.20 per hour would be appropriate. Therefore:

2 cleaning staff for 2 hours per evening = 4 hours per evening
4 hours per evening × 5 days per week = 20 hours' cleaning time per week
20 hours cleaning × £9.20 per hour = £184 per week

Next, convert this to a monthly price. You should work from a calendar month price because this will give you the same price for each month regardless of the days within the month. Therefore:

£184 × 56.8 weeks = £10,451.20
£10,451.20 ÷ 12 = £870.93

Your quote, therefore, would be £858.67 per calender month plus VAT (if applicable).

You must allow for an additional 4.8 weeks in the year to cover the four weeks' holiday you will have to pay your employees (correct at the time of writing).

SENDING YOUR QUOTE

Send your quote by email. This is by far the quickest and best method, and most clients prefer to receive quotes this way. The example quote given in Figure 6 (created in Microsoft Word) should cover all the key information you need to provide. As a further professional touch, convert the document to a PDF file, which will make it look better. You can convert documents for free at various websites. The following two are recommended:

☐ www.pdfonline.com
☐ www.freepdfconvert.com

Cleaning Quote

Your details	
Company	Z Ltd
Contact	Mr Pearson
Address	Unit 7, Fairfield Business Centre, Birmingham BXX 6XX
Telephone	0800 123 456

Quote summary	
Location of service	As above
Days per week	5 days per week – Monday to Friday
No of cleaners	2 cleaners
Supervising cleaner	One cleaner to be recognized supervisor
Cleaning duration	2 hours per clean
a.m. or p.m. clean	p.m. clean – 6 to 8
Cleaning supplies	All basic supplies included in quote
Consumables	Toilet rolls, bin liners are chargeable – price list available
Start date	Monday 10 September
Access details	Key access with alarm codes

Notes on premises
Having visited your premises we can see there is definite room for improvement in the cleaning standards. We propose to offer you higher standards of cleaning, better consistency and reliability and, in general, we feel that our personalized cleaning schedule will meet and exceed all your expectations of a cleaning service.

Quote 1
£858.67
Summary: 2 cleaners for 2 hours per evening, 5 days per week
All quotes are subject to VAT
Invoicing is at the beginning of each month on 30-day terms
Quotes are calculated on a per calendar month basis – some quotes are calculated on a 4-weekly basis. Please check this when comparing quotes.

Fig. 6. Cleaning quote

While the quote in Figure 6 should be adequate, you may wish to add some further information to this. The following could be used to support your quote or to provide your client with information they may find helpful:

☐ Company policies, including health and safety and environmental issues.

☐ A list of the other services you provide.

☐ Information on the management and auditing of cleaning accounts.

☐ Any general information that may support or complement your quote.

Arranging the start date and next meeting

Your quote has been successful, and Z Ltd have given their current cleaning company one month's notice. Your start date, therefore, will be Monday, 10 September. This gives you ample time to plan things at your end.

The next stage is to arrange a further meeting. Hold this in the week prior to the start date. This will keep things fresh and will get the ball rolling in anticipation of the start date. You should, therefore, arrange a meeting with Z Ltd on Tuesday, 4 September. In this meeting you should:

☐ finalize the start time for the cleaning staff;

☐ discuss entry procedures and alarm codes and access;

☐ discuss the cleaning schedule for each day;

☐ find out where the cleaning storage area will be;

☐ find out where the refuse sacks are taken (to the front of building, the car park, etc.);

☐ find out about any quirks, such as internal offices that are always locked; and

☐ generally chat and begin the all-important relationship building with your new client.

This meeting should be kept fairly short – just long enough for you to find out all the information you need before the start date.

Setting the cleaning schedules

Now that you have established the cleaning schedule, you should translate this into a printable schedule that is easy to read and understand by both your client and staff. Try to keep this schedule to one page.

The schedule should contain the following key elements:

☐ The basic daily duties.

☐ The detail cleaning duties.

☐ Any special client requests (e.g. the fridge cleaned on a Monday).

Figure 7 on page 76 is an example cleaning schedule that covers all the basics. This schedule is straightforward to create using Microsoft Word, and you can use the same template over and over again, simply customizing it for each of your clients.

Once you have prepared the cleaning schedule, you should present it to your client for their feedback. After reading this, your client may want to change it and, if they do, you will have to incorporate these changes into the schedule. Once your client is happy with the schedule, you are ready to move on to the next stage.

Preparing welcome packs

You should prepare a welcome pack for your client. While this may include the same things that were in your presentation folder, to be thorough it should contain the following as a minimum:

☐ A welcome note.

☐ A priority contact list.

☐ A copy of the cleaning schedule.

☐ A copy of your insurance.

☐ The service agreement.

☐ A risk assessment and methods statement.

☐ Brief environmental, equal opportunities and health and safety policies.

☐ A list of your additional services (if you choose to have any).

WELCOME NOTE

All this need entail is a short paragraph or two thanking your client for choosing your company and a brief mission statement.

PRIORITY CONTACT LIST

Provide contact details through which your client may reach you, including your office, mobile and fax numbers and your email address. It is worthwhile noting on the contact list that calls are accepted any time of the day.

A COPY OF THE CLEANING SCHEDULE

This if for your client to keep for reference.

MONDAY	Collect all dishes and place in dishwasher	Empty all waste baskets	Vacuum all carpets	Dust all over, inc. desks	Wet mop all hard floors	Fully clean kitchen, including sink area	Fully clean and restock toilets	Polish aluminium	Clean fridge out	Spot/detail clean toilets
TUESDAY	Collect all dishes and place in dishwasher	Empty all waste baskets	Vacuum all carpets	Dust all over, inc. desks	Wet mop all hard floors	Fully clean kitchen, including sink area	Fully clean and restock toilets	Polish brass and copper	Wet wipe waste baskets	Spot/detail clean kitchen
WEDNESDAY	Collect all dishes and place in dishwasher	Empty all waste baskets	Vacuum all carpets	Dust all over, inc. desks	Wet mop all hard floors	Fully clean kitchen, including sink area	Fully clean and restock toilets	Clean partition glass	High-level dust all over	Spot/detail clean office area
THURSDAY	Collect all dishes and place in dishwasher	Empty all waste baskets	Vacuum all carpets	Dust all over, inc. desks	Wet mop all hard floors	Fully clean kitchen, including sink area	Fully clean and restock toilets	Clean around all skirting	Vacuum all seats	Vertical spot clean all over
FRIDAY	Collect all dishes and place in dishwasher	Empty all waste baskets	Vacuum all carpets	Dust all over, inc. desks	Wet mop all hard floors	Fully clean kitchen, including sink area	Fully clean and restock toilets	Clean all windowsills	Wipe all seat and desk legs	

Fig. 7 Cleaning schedule

A COPY OF YOUR INSURANCE

Your client will require a copy of your insurance for their health and safety records and also as evidence of your legitimacy and integrity as a company.

THE SERVICE AGREEMENT

You should include some form of agreement your client can sign and return. This should set out the following:

☐ That the agreement will last for one year on a rolling basis.

☐ That the client cannot steal your cleaning staff and then dismiss your company.

☐ That the client agrees to pay the agreed quote price each month.

☐ That the client agrees to increases in the price where these are unavoidable (e.g. increases to the national minimum wage).

☐ The notice period your client must provide you.

You should take professional advice on the contents and wording of this agreement, particularly as your company and number of clients grow.

A RISK ASSESSMENT AND METHOD STATEMENT

Health and safety is of vital importance. While a standard risk assessment and method statement may suffice, you may again wish to seek professional advice on this. Alternatively, if you search the Internet, you should find templates you can modify to suit your own needs.

BRIEF ENVIRONMENTAL, EQUAL OPPORTUNITIES AND HEALTH AND SAFETY POLICIES

Similarly, you may wish to seek professional advice on these or you may want to produce your own. You should, however, keep these brief – ideally one page, if possible.

A LIST OF YOUR ADDITIONAL SERVICES

Promote your business at every available turn. Including a list of any additional services you offer in your welcome pack is simply another opportunity to sell your business.

Organizing your staff

A word of warning: don't leave it until the last minute to organize your cleaning staff – you will suffer the consequences if you do!

Z Ltd require two cleaning staff. A hard-and-fast rule is that any account that requires more than one cleaner should have a recognized cleaning supervisor. For this account, therefore, you will need one recognized supervisor and one general cleaner. The supervisor will be a working cleaner but they will be paid more and will have extra responsibilities for running the account:

☐ Ensuring the detail cleaning is carried out.

☐ Making sure the cleaning time is fulfilled.

☐ Ensuring stock is ordered as required.

☐ Reporting staff issues and problems (lateness, sickness, holidays, etc.).

☐ Dealing with any daily onsite client liaison.

☐ Generally being your eyes and ears on the job.

Once you have chosen two members of staff, you should make it clear to them what time they must arrive and how they should dress. Keep in regular contact with them all the way to the start-point because, as has been noted elsewhere, cleaning staff have a way of letting you down!

Preparing your cleaning materials

Your quote will have allowed for all the basic cleaning supplies, machinery and uniforms the account requires:

☐ vacuum

☐ mops/buckets

☐ cloths and dusters

☐ general cleaning chemicals

☐ tabard or full uniform.

The vacuum will be the most expensive item you supply. For small accounts, however, you may be able to use the client's own vacuum cleaner.

You should not supply any of the following consumable items unless you have specifically factored them into your quote as an additional cost:

☐ Toilet rolls.

☐ Bin liners.

☐ Black bags or council refuse sacks.

☐ Hand towels, centre-pull or other paper products.

☐ Dishwasher tablets or washing-up liquid.

Consumable items such as these are an ideal source of extra revenue. It is worthwhile, therefore, to encourage your clients to let you supply these and to charge accordingly.

Starting the first shift

Aim to arrive between half and hour to an hour before the cleaning shift's start time. Have the cleaning staff arrive early also. This will give you time to unpack and store all your cleaning materials in your designated area and to discuss the cleaning schedule with your staff.

It is a good idea at this stage to walk the premises to show your staff exactly what each job entails. For example, the cleaning schedule says: 'Vacuum all the carpets.' You could say to your cleaning staff:

> *I want you to vacuum all these carpets. Be sure to get under these desks and to pull out these chairs to get good access. Make sure you put the chairs back and also keep an eye on this shredder area as there will be lots of paper cuttings . . .*

In general, you should use this time with your staff to emphasize some important points:

☐ Show them the cleaning staff cupboard and stress that it must be kept tidy.

☐ Go through the schedule to clarify all areas.

☐ Go through key access and alarm procedures. It is very important this is done correctly.

☐ Show them where the refuse sacks or bulk rubbish go.

☐ Go through any specific points, such as tricky keys or locked offices.

☐ Point out areas of detail cleaning to pay attention to.

☐ Generally underline the importance of standards, reliability and consistency.

It is strongly advised that you stay with your staff for the complete shift. This will allow you to assess them as they work. It is also advisable to become involved with the cleaning on this first shift, so dress formally but comfortably and show the staff you don't mind getting your hands dirty. This will earn you the respect of your employees and will give you a hands on feel for the requirements of the work.

Once the shift is over, take a good walk round the premises and make sure nothing has been missed. Check for missed bins, cups still in the sink, rooms not locked and lights left on. All these things are regular misses, and it will help if your staff walk round with you. Direct most of your comments to the supervisor because this is the person whom you will rely on to do this in your absence.

When the shift is over and you are happy all is complete, let the supervisor lock up and put the alarm code on so that you are happy they can do this. Thank the staff for their hard work and tell them you will see them tomorrow evening.

Following up

The next day you should give your client either an early-morning visit or an early-morning courtesy call. Ask them if all looked well this morning and if there is anything that has been missed. This conscientious approach will reflect well on you, and your client will feel they have someone who takes pride in their work and who wants to provide a good service.

If the client tells you that a bin was missed and the dishwasher wasn't put on, you should immediately offer to go round to rectify these problems. More often than not they will not mind because teething problems are inevitable, but you should offer, none the less.

Presuming all has gone well, you should pass this information on to your cleaning staff the next evening. Congratulate and thank them for a great start. Remember, good work should always be recognized, whenever possible. For the next two weeks you should visit the account every other night to check everything is in order. Follow this with a minimum of fortnightly checks.

7

ENSURING QUALITY OF SERVICE

❨ *To give real service you must add something which cannot be bought or measured with money, and that is sincerity and integrity* ❩

(Douglas Adams, author and satirist)

This chapter discusses those things that will ensure you provide your clients with a quality service. It is, therefore, appropriate to begin this chapter with guidance from the British Institute of Cleaning Sciences' (BICSc) code of practice – BICSc, after all, is the standard bearer for the cleaning industry: A corporate member of BICSc should:

☐ maintain a high standard of integrity in all their working relationships, whether inside or outside the organization in which they are employed;

☐ foster the highest possible competence and expertise among those for whom they may be responsible;

☐ seek to take a positive role in institute national and branch affairs by attending meetings and assisting in appropriate ways at branch and national events;

☐ support such events and encourage staff to participate in them;

☐ comply with both the letter and spirit of the appropriate legislation of the country in which they work;

☐ discharge any obligations into which they may have entered in the course of their employment or matters of business;

☐ reject working practices that might reasonably be deemed improper;

☐ ensure the availability of appropriate training for any staff under their control and encourage staff to take part in such training;

☐ raise their own standards of professional competence by taking advantage of any training that may be made available;

☐ declare any personal interest that may conflict or might be deemed by others to conflict with their impartiality in commercial employment or contractual matters or in institute affairs; and

☐ not divulge any confidential information that may be received in the course of employment or institute affairs and not seek to use such information to their personal advantage.

Providing your clients with a service

As noted on many occasions in this book, clients are your business. Keeping your clients is equally as important as finding new ones, and you can only retain your clients through good and consistent levels of service. When clients choose a service provider, they do not anticipate cancelling the contract after a few months or a year or so – they take on a cleaning company in the belief it will be a good service provider. It is when things go wrong that a client will consider cancelling a cleaning contract. It is up to you, therefore, whether you retain or lose your clients.

First, deliver what you promise: if you cannot deliver it, do not promise it! Remember, most clients only require the following from a cleaning service:

☐ Clean premises every day.

☐ A competitive price.

☐ An understanding of their needs and expectations – you understand not only your own business but also theirs.

☐ A consistent cleaning service: same cleaner, no days missed.

☐ To be kept informed.

☐ That comments, queries and complaints are dealt with and rectified the first time of asking.

☐ Support and attention, when required.

In most cases, if you attend to these requirements, you will retain your clients. Despite your best efforts, however, there will be occasions when your relationship with a client breaks down:

☐ You underestimated the cleaning time. As a result, you are struggling to achieve quality with the labour budget available.

☐ The client may have unreasonable and demanding expectations.

☐ You have committed yourself to a task you are untrained to do or are incapable of carrying out.

☐ The client's premises are in an area where it is difficult to find cleaning staff willing to travel there.

☐ The client does not tell you about the problems they are having with your service and cancels out of the blue without giving you an opportunity to rectify these problems.

☐ The client is experiencing financial problems and wants to cancel the cleaning contract to ease their financial burden.

While there is little you can do to avoid the above, the point remains that you should never compromise on your level of client service.

The following are ten tips on how to deliver a great service:

1. The quality of your service is directly related to the quality of the cleaning staff who deliver it. Remember this when you are considering paying your staff low wages, or when you decide not to train them or not to reward effort.

2. If you treat your staff well and if your staff see that you care about your clients, this will rub off on your staff. Come across as lazy, abusive and uninterested, however, and your staff will be lazy, abusive and uninterested.

3. Get to know your clients. Remember their names and any comments they make, such as about their children, hobbies or interests. When you ask them about their children or a particular hobby or interest, they will note this: play to people's interests.

4. Similarly, let your clients get to know you. Whether you have achieved this or not will show if you are able to discuss topics other than cleaning.

5. Go that extra mile: a birthday card, a compliment, a Christmas present. Break down the barriers between you and your client and they will be less inclined to get rid of you.

6. Acknowledge your client's position of power over you. Play on your client's vanity to some extent: acknowledge them as your employer.

7. Agree even when you disagree, particularly on issues that do not affect your service. Being argumentative and opinionated for the sake of it will achieve nothing.

8. Bend the rules slightly to ingratiate yourself with your client. The end result will be that your client will feel as though they have received 'special' treatment. Plant the seeds of a strong, long-term relationship ('I should not really give you this price because it is cheaper than the one I charge other clients').

9. Train your cleaning staff in how to deal with your clients. Some things will look good if they come from a member of your cleaning staff; on the other hand, there are some things your cleaning staff should not say to your clients.

10. Invite comments. Ask your clients for their thoughts and feelings about your cleaning service. This may seem like putting yourself in the firing line, but it is better to know about problems and to deal with them than not to know and lose a client.

Auditing

Audits are a formal, professional way to monitor not only cleaning standards but also your client's state of mind. Both these aspects are very important. Audits should be carried out every two weeks and should follow the process shown in Figure 8. This is a continuous process and, as long as you follow it diligently, you will not only appear to be very efficient but your cleaning staff will also get the message about the expectations you have of the cleaning – they will pick up and rectify those things repeatedly found wrong in the audits.

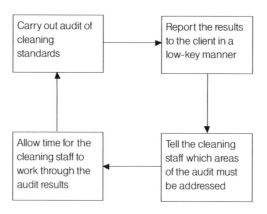

Fig. 8. The audit process

You should create an audit sheet containing fields you can complete as you carry out the audit. If you have these printed professionally, you will be able to order duplicate or triplicate self-carbonating pads so that you can leave copies of your audits with your client and/or cleaner. To begin with, however, it may be more economical to print your own. Figure 9 is an example of an audit sheet. This contains sections that should cover most of the areas you would want to audit. Your client should sign and date the last section to confirm they are satisfied (or not) with the standards of service.

Producing detail lists

Detail lists are a way of passing information quickly to your cleaning staff. They may be made as a result of an informal visit either during cleaning hours or at some other time. You may, for example, have popped in for a short chat with your staff and, during your visit, you notice some areas that look as though they require attention. Instead of doing a formal audit, you should use this opportunity to have a brief 'walkabout' with the supervising cleaner.

A detail list is a sheet of paper on which you can jot down areas you found on the walkabout that need attention. After you have discussed the issues noted with your staff, you should make a copy of the detail list and leave it with the member of staff with a target date for completion. Always date, therefore, the top of the sheet. After a few days when you next visit, the work may all be complete or a number of items may have been ticked by the member of staff as they work through the list. If nothing has been done after a few days, then there should be a very good reason for this! Figure 10 on page 86 is an example of a simple detail list.

Account Audit Sheet

The Cleaning Company

Account	Audit report	Areas not addressed from previous visit
Address	General areas	
Audit date		
Service manager		
	Toilet areas	Client feedback

Cleaners' area

	Yes	No
Cleaning area tidy?	☐	☐
Equipment clean?	☐	☐
Equipment in good condition?	☐	☐
Appropriate chemicals?	☐	☐
Staff wearing uniforms?	☐	☐
Colour coding in place?	☐	☐
Cleaning schedule in place?	☐	☐

Kitchen areas

I consider the current level of service to be

Excellent ☐ Good ☐ Acceptable ☐ Unacceptable ☐

I would like more attention given to the following areas:

Further comments

Sign . . . .

Print Name . . . .

Position . . . .

Date . . . .

Fig. 9. Audit sheet

```
Detail cleaning list - 12/09/xx

Desk legs dusty
Vacuum under desks
High=level dusting required
Fridge needs cleaning out
Sink splashback needs cleaning
Door glass needs cleaning
Underside of toilet pans need cleaning
Clean out cutlery drawer
Clean inside microwave
Dust behind computer monitors
Cleaners' area needs tidying
```

Fig. 10. Detail list

The importance of following up

If you do not instigate a process of follow-up for all aspects of your service, any efforts with regards to audits and detail lists will be pointless. There are two different ways to follow up.

CLEANING STAFF FOLLOW-UP

The only way to know that something has been done to the required standard is to check it with your own eyes. Even if you have been told something has been done, you should take all reasonable steps to verify this for yourself – only then will you have the peace of mind that positive action has being taken.

The follow-up process for audits, detail lists and general checks is the same:

☐ Return with your copy of the list of areas to be attended to.

☐ Speak to the cleaning staff or supervisor. Check they have their copy of this list. If not, they are not giving due attention to your instructions.

☐ Explain you are there to follow up on this list. Get some feedback from them – you can be sure they will have some!

☐ Walk round and check every item on the list with, if possible, the member of staff responsible for that item.

☐ Give your staff feedback on the results of this check – both positive and negative.

□ Suggest ways the speed or standard of the work could be improved – make constructive comments.

□ Do not resort to anger or shout tactics if the results are not as you expected. Ask simple probing questions to find out why the work has not been done properly.

CLIENT FOLLOW-UP

If you have no follow-up process in place to check your staff have acted on simple instructions your client has given you and that you have passed on to your staff (such as there is some additional rubbish to be thrown out or the rubbish bags are to go in a different place), what started as a simple instruction from your client may build up to a complaint if the instruction is not carried out correctly. Do not rely on your staff's say so – check for yourself.

Having the right attitude

No matter what other qualities you may have, such as patience or intelligence, these will be of little value if you do not have the right attitude towards your clients. Most of your clients will initially be strangers to you, and you will normally have only a short period of time in which to communicate with them. Make the best use of this time. For example, if you are angry about something, this will usually show itself in the way you behave towards other people; similarly, if you are ecstatically happy, people will see this in your attitude.

You should, therefore, always try to be professional in your approach to your clients: put aside feelings and emotions that will affect your attitude negatively. Your personal problems are not something a client wants or needs to hear about. Try always to be positive. This will not only rub off on other people but it will also help your mental well-being. The following are some tips to help you maintain a positive attitude when all around you seems to be awry:

□ **Have balance in your life**. A settled home life should mean your work life is more balanced and less hectic. Upheavals and dramas in your personal life will show in your attitude to your work.

□ **Never give up**. Every problem has its solution, and mistakes should be regarded as a learning process, not as an indication you should give up.

□ **Make the best of a situation**. Try to identify those things that are making you unhappy and look for ways to improve, avoid or manage them.

□ **Think positively**. Believe in yourself – positive thinking is a key ingredient of success. Do not entertain negative thoughts.

□ **Visualize success**. Apply your mind to those things that will enable you to succeed. This mental preparation will help you to make the most of those situations that will lead to success.

- ☐ **Face your problems**. Problems do not simply disappear, and solutions to problems are usually much easier to achieve than you may think. Tackle your problems head on.

- ☐ **Always look on the bright side**. Look for the positives in a situation and draw on these.

- ☐ **Don't lose your sense of humour**. People don't like to be with someone who is miserable. Don't take little things too seriously – look for the humour in a situation as opposed to the negatives.

- ☐ **Put some fun into your work**. Within reason, try to inject mundane and boring activities with something interesting.

- ☐ **Play on the positives**. Identify your positives and bring these to the front; identify your weaknesses and work on turning these into positives.

Conduct and ethics

Conduct and ethics go hand in hand. Conduct covers not only the way you behave but also the way you fulfil (or not) the legal obligations you have towards your staff, for example. Most large companies have a business code of conduct in which they outline their responsibilities and obligations to both their staff and clients. While you may not have a formal code of conduct yourself, you should always deal with your staff and clients in a moral and ethical way. This is yet another step towards your overall goal of controlling both the quality and service of your business.

The Institute of Business Ethics (IBE) was established solely 'to encourage high standards of business behaviour based on ethical values'. The IBE offers the following ten practical rules for good business conduct:

- ☐ Establish your core business values and stick to them or else your reputation will suffer.

- ☐ The welfare and motivation of your staff are critical to your success.

- ☐ Remember that the owner-manager's business behaviour will be taken as a role model by the staff.

- ☐ If you need a partner in your business, make sure they share both your vision and values.

- ☐ Work at your relations with your clients – they neither start nor stop when the sale is made.

- ☐ Don't knock your competitors.

- ☐ Stick to your agreed terms of payment.

- ☐ Record all financial transactions in your books.

☐ Find at least one way of supporting the communities in which you operate.

☐ If you are doubtful about an ethical issue in your business, take advice.

Good business practice will reflect well on your business. Remember also the following:

☐ **First impressions count**. You may have heard the saying: 'You never get a second chance to make a first impression.' First impressions can make or break you, so always be alert and professional.

☐ **Work on your public relations skills**. While public relations are usually associated with large companies, the way you conduct and deliver yourself is a public relations exercise. If you have a good image, your company will also have a good image.

☐ **Be naturally confident**. People who are naturally confident inspire the confidence of others. When a potential client sees your confidence and the faith you have in your ability to deliver a quality service, they will take confidence from this that you are the person for the job.

☐ **Be attractive**. If you present yourself well, if you speak to individuals and groups in an interesting and effective way, if you look others in the eye when speaking – all these will be regarded by others as your attractive features. Work on being attractive to others.

☐ **Have good manners**. Well mannered people are generally appreciated. A simple 'Thank you' or 'Sorry' will make an immediate difference to how people see you as a person.

Application

From a service point of view, 'application' is defined as 'a diligent effort, a job that requires serious application'. The success of your company depends on the application you are prepared to put in to achieving this success. The following are some key areas you should continually apply yourself to in order to achieve success:

☐ **Advertising**: to bring in new clients.

☐ **Recruitment and employment practices**: to find and keep good-quality staff.

☐ **Standards**: to achieve consistently high standards.

☐ **Training**: to make the time to educate and inform.

☐ **Innovation**: to look constantly for new ways to improve all aspects of your business.

☐ **Bookkeeping**: to account for your business transactions and to pay your taxes.

☐ **Problem-solving**: to deal with problems as they arise.

☐ **Debt chasing**: to make sure you are paid all monies owed you. As your business grows this will become an area that requires constant application.

☐ **Financial control**: to control sales, overheads, margins and profits.

All these items require a continuous cycle of application. As noted elsewhere in this book, being self-employed is a 24-hour, seven days a week business. If your last thoughts at night and first thoughts in the morning concern any of these areas, this is a good indication your mental application is correct. This is, however, only part of the story: application in theory is a great deal easier than application in practice.

Successful people have acquired the ability to turn application in theory to application in practice. Notice the word 'acquired' here. While some people may have this ability naturally, it can also be learnt and developed through application itself. All these people understand that you only get out of something what you put into it. The people who apply themselves and who have achieved success, therefore, all share similar traits. They:

☐ are focused;

☐ have vision and know what they want to achieve;

☐ are positive thinkers;

☐ swoop on opportunities when they find them;

☐ learn from mistakes and failures and move on;

☐ solve problems and break down the obstacles towards success;

☐ have faith in their ideas; and

☐ never quit.

Never relent in your application: in time, you will fulfil your ambitions.

Dealing with staff problems

Ninety per cent of your problems will lie with your cleaning staff. While you may often feel a degree of loathing towards them, try to keep this to yourself. As noted on many occasions in this book, your cleaning staff may let you down in more ways than you can imagine, so you should try to hold on to those members of staff who are intelligent, hard-working, honest and well presented.

Among the problems you may experience are staff being badly presented and spoken; poor attendance and application; staff throwing away items that should not have been thrown away; stealing or accusations of stealing from clients' offices; and fighting in clients' premises – the list is endless. There is, unfortunately, not one solution to all these problems, but there are various measures you can take to deal with each:

☐ **Interviews**: the more interviews you hold, the bigger the pool of cleaning staff you will be able to choose from. At the very least, interviews give you the opportunity to choose the best from what may be a bad bunch.

- ☐ **Terms and conditions**: set the terms and conditions of employment that your employees must sign. These should cover the basic requirements of the job, including attendance, presentation and application, etc. Give your employees a copy of these requirements to read and keep.

- ☐ **Induction**: induct your employees not only about the cleaning account they will be working on but also about your company's basic expectations. This will make it clear to your employees about what is and what is not allowed.

- ☐ **Audits and follow-ups**: follow the audit procedure set out earlier in this chapter. This will help to solve such problems as poor standards and poor application.

- ☐ **Spot checks**: spot checks will reveal such problems as cleaning staff leaving their shifts early, opportunities for thefts, unscheduled breaks and skiving.

- ☐ **Training**: training will help you to identify areas of weakness in your cleaning staff and to improve these. It will also help to motivate your staff because they will learn new skills. Similarly, training will give you the opportunity to identify those employees who want to learn and those who do *not* want to learn and who may be having a negative affect on other members of your staff.

- ☐ **Meetings**: there is nothing more disconcerting than tackling a bunch of irate people in one go. Deal with your cleaning staff one to one. You will then be able to enforce yourself and your point to greater affect.

- ☐ **Maintain contact**: phone your staff regularly. Let them hear your voice and your enthusiasm for the service you are providing. When they feel isolated, staff can become jaded and unmotivated.

- ☐ **Recognition and motivation**: your staff may seem unmotivated, but the challenge is there – do your best to make them better. You will be surprised with the results if you recognize effort and motivate the weaker members of your staff.

No shows

While some of the above problems may not cause too much trouble or may perhaps go unnoticed, no shows can, and will, cause major logistical and operational problems, not only to the running of your business but also to your personal life. Imagine you receive a call from a client on a Tuesday morning at 8.15 a.m. to tell you their office was not cleaned the night before. Imagine that same client has had to do this more than once – perhaps even a few times. Now imagine losing that client, because this is what will happen.

A great many cleaning staff take time off as they see fit, and the reasons they give for this will be a mixture of truth and lies. Cleaning staff will often not show up for work and they may not inform you about this beforehand. While you should consider the reasons behind any particular absence, cleaners who are regularly absent are unacceptable and you should replace them as soon as you can.

Be particularly wary of weekend shifts and be prepared for that call on a Sunday morning telling you that so and so will not be in to work today because they, or someone they know, is sick or there are transport problems. For some reason, staff will never say they cannot come in to work because they have a hangover!

So, what is the solution? You cannot, of course, force every member of staff to follow a procedure for calling in when absent, and, to a certain degree, you will just have to accept that this goes with the territory. Something you should consider, however, and this should be incorporated into your employees' terms and condition of employment, is a set schedule people must follow in the event of any absence. Staff who call you first to let you know of their impending absence at least give you a chance to find cover so that the shift is not missed. The more notice they give, the better. With such a system in place, you could even tolerate, on rare occasions, extremely short-notice absences.

Such a system will not cure the problem but it will give you the peace of mind that, in the event of a let-down, you have pointed out to your staff the requirements for absence and that there can be no excuses when disciplinary action is taken. An example of such a schedule is as follows. The minimum notice required for an absence is:

☐ for one day off – three days' notice;

☐ for two days or more off – one week's notice;

☐ for one week off – two weeks' notice; and

☐ for more than one week off – four weeks' notice.

You may also want to initiate a process of telephoning your employees before each shift. This could simply be a matter of saying: 'Hi, Joan, just checking you are OK for your shifts. I'm trying to make sure nobody lets me down this weekend.' As your staff levels grow, however, this may not always be practical but, in the first year, it is a good procedure to follow because it will give you the peace of mind you desire, particularly when you are looking forward to a weekend off! You are also putting discreet pressure on the person to attend their shift: they have spoken to you and know they will be letting you down if they do not turn up. Use all the tools you have at your disposal to achieve your goals – including psychology.

Be proactive and reactive

To be a reactive manager these days carries many negative connotations: people say you should be proactive, not reactive. While this may be true in some situations, you should also be aware that, when it comes to running a service business and, in particular, a cleaning business, both attributes are required.

First, we should understand the difference between the words 'proactive' and 'reactive'. Proactive means to act in advance to deal with an expected difficulty – in other words, to be anticipatory. Reactive means to be responsive or to react to an incident. To be proactive is, therefore, to act in advance of a problem occurring. To be reactive, on the other hand, is to deal with a problem swiftly after it has occurred. This is why we are always being told to think proactively, to manage proactively and to encourage our employees to act proactively.

This is sound advice: at every opportunity you should be proactive in your approach. Audits, detail lists, follow-ups and application are all proactive measures you can take to improve the quality of your service provision. However, you can never be proactive to the point where problems no longer occur. Proactivity will reduce the number of problems that are likely to occur but, as cleaning is a problem business, dealing with problems is simply part and parcel of running such a business.

Bearing this in mind, you will see that to be reactive is equally, if not more, important as being proactive: when problems occur, you must be reactive in dealing with them. For example, if you do not respond immediately to a client's problem, not only are you not being 'reactive' but also all your proactive work will count for nothing.

The following are the qualities of both a proactive and reactive manager. A proactive manager:

☐ has a thoughtful and analytic approach;

☐ is not perturbed by 'panic' or 'emergency' situations;

☐ can see the bigger picture;

☐ can identify the causes of repeat failures and non-performances;

☐ focuses on the root of a problem, not on the surface level; and

☐ sees a task to the end and is not lost in the details.

A reactive manager:

☐ is efficient, fast and decisive in dealing with problems;

☐ thinks logically and directs others who are struggling to cope with urgent issues;

☐ is good at finding answers to situations and problems as they arrive;

☐ is innovative and can find new solutions to old problems; and

☐ is in control and can inspire confidence in clients and employees.

It is through being reactive that you will learn to be proactive. The following, therefore, are a further few tips to help you develop a proactive management style:

☐ Take some time out – without interruptions – to be with your own thoughts.

☐ Examine each problem separately, starting with the biggest.

☐ Try to establish how often the problem is occurring.

☐ Look at the source of the problem.

☐ Find out if there are any prior indications that the problem is about to happen.

☐ Consider what methods you used previously to resolve the problem and whether these can be improved.

☐ Take a broad look: ask yourself how the problem could have been prevented.

☐ Put a proactive plan in place to avoid the problem happening again.

☐ Instigate a monitoring procedure that can alert you to the warning signs.

☐ Try to resolve the problem before it escalates.

8

HEALTH AND SAFETY, LAWS AND REGULATIONS

❪ Good people do not need laws to tell them to act responsibly, while bad people will find a way around the laws ❫

(Plato, Greek philosopher)

This chapter looks at the health and safety requirements, laws and regulations that will affect you, not only when you start your company but also when your business grows. These are inescapable things every reputable company must comply with. Do not, therefore, cut corners because this would lead not only to client losses but also, potentially, to legal action against you.

Planning for health and safety

Health and safety requirements apply to almost everyone who works: employees themselves, the self-employed, young people on work experience, apprentices, etc. The following are the basic health and safety requirements that will affect you. First, under the Health and Safety at Work, etc. Act 1974:

☐ Employers must ensure their employees and anyone else who could be affected by their work (such as visitors, members of the public, patients, etc.) are kept safe from harm and that their health is not affected. This means slip and trip risks must be controlled to ensure people do not slip, trip or fall.

☐ Employees must use any safety equipment provided and must not cause danger to themselves or others.

☐ Manufacturers and suppliers must ensure that their products are safe. They must also provide information about their appropriate use.

Secondly, the Management of Health and Safety at Work Regulations 1999 build on the requirements of this Act to include duties on employers to assess risks (including slip and trip risks) and, where necessary, to take action to safeguard health and safety. Finally, the Workplace (Health, Safety and Welfare) Regulations 1992 require that floors are suitable for the workplace and for the work activity, and that they are kept in good condition and free from obstructions. People must also be able to move around safely.

Controlling for the risk of danger is no different from any other task – you should identify the risks, decide what to do about them and take action to reduce them. The following are the 10 key things you must do to comply with health and safety requirements:

1. Identify those areas of your work that could cause harm to people and decide which precautions to take to prevent this harm from happening. This is your risk assessment.

2. Decide how you are going to manage health and safety in your business. If you have five or more employees, you must write this down. This is your health and safety policy.

3. If you employ anyone at all, you will need employers' liability insurance. You must display the certificate of this in your workplace.

4. You must provide free health and safety training for your workers so they know what hazards and risks they may face and how to deal with them.

5. You must obtain competent advice about your health and safety duties. This can come from workers in your business, external consultants/advisers or a combination of these.

6. You must provide toilets, washing facilities and drinking water for all your employees, including those with disabilities. These are your employees' basic health, safety and welfare needs.

7. You must consult your employees on health and safety matters.

8. If you employ anyone at all, you must display the health and safety law poster or provide your workers with a leaflet containing the same information.

9. If you are an employer, self-employed or in control of work premises, by law you must report certain work-related accidents, diseases and dangerous occurrences to the Health and Safety Executive (HSE) or your local authority.

10. If you are a new business, you must register with either the HSE or your local authority, depending on the sort of business you have.

Accidents to cleaners

In 2005–6, approximately 3,500 work-related accidents to cleaners were reported to the HSE and local authorities. Over 700 of these accidents were classified as major injuries (for example, dislocations or broken bones). The most common types of accidents reported were:

☐ slips and trips;

☐ manual handling injuries; and

☐ falls from a height.

The main health risks affecting the cleaning industry are injuries to the back and upper limbs and occupational dermatitis. Figure 11 shows the major accidents to cleaners for the period 2003–6. As you will see, slips and trips are by far and away the most common cause of accidents.

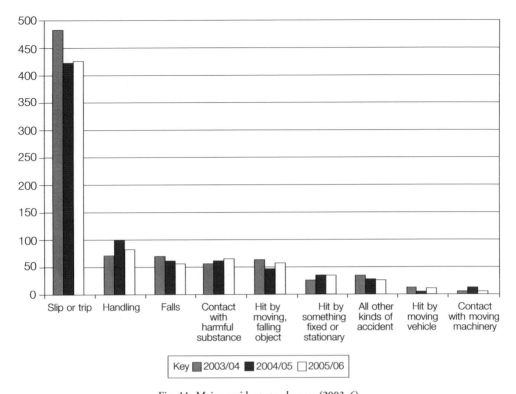

Fig. 11. Major accidents to cleaners (2003–6)

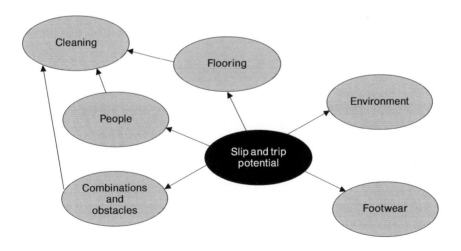

Fig. 12. Major causes of trip and slip accidents

Slip and trip accidents happen for a number of reasons, and Figure 12 on page 97 should help you to understand what causes them. The bubbles highlight the main factors that contribute to a slip and trip accident. One or more of these factors may play a part in any accident.

To safeguard against slip and trip accidents, you should:

☐ have in place an effective management system;

☐ carry out regular risk assessments; and

☐ make sure you are aware of the relevant laws and regulations.

The following are five tips that should help prevent slips and trips:

1. **Plan**: work with your employees to identify potential problem areas and set goals for their improvement.

2. **Train**: give your employees the knowledge to identify and to take action over potential risks.

3. **Organize**: make your employees, including your cleaning and contract staff, responsible for specific areas.

4. **Control**: ensure working practices and processes are being carried out properly and keep a record of all cleaning and maintenance work.

5. **Monitor and review**: talk to your employees so they can feed back on how the measures are working.

If you instigate good working practices and exercise due diligence, you should find that accidents are few and far between.

Complying with employment law

Even though a great deal of employment law does not apply to small businesses, there are certain areas of this complex legislation you must comply with. To do this, you should keep in touch with developments and should try to implement good-practice policies. There are six areas of employment law you should be aware of:

1. recruitment;

2. hours, leave and pay;

3. employee rights;

4. discrimination and equal opportunities;

5. sickness; and

6. disciplinary issues.

RECRUITMENT

Discrimination of any kind is illegal – you should assess employees solely on their abilities to carry out the requirements of a job. When you interview applicants for a job, make notes about what was said during the interview: applicants have a legal right to request copies of these notes. Remember also that a contract of employment begins as soon as your job offer is accepted, whether this offer was made verbally or in writing. Therefore:

☐ Do not intimate to an applicant during an interview that you are offering them a job.

☐ When you do offer someone a job, do this in writing and inform the applicant that the position is subject to terms and conditions that will be provided later.

☐ Cover yourself if you are waiting for references. Tell the applicant that your offer of employment is subject to you receiving satisfactory references.

A written statement of the terms and conditions of employment must be provided within the first two months of the person starting the job. These must specify certain details about the job, such as hours, pay and entitlements, etc. You have the right, however, to amend the job description if required and to change the employee's place of work, but you must obtain the employee's consent to do this. Otherwise, this would be breach of contract. Also, make sure that your disciplinary procedure is up to date and in conformance with statutory minimum requirements.

HOURS, LEAVE AND PAY

There are statutory requirements concerning working time. For example, most employees are entitled to work for a maximum of 48 hours per week only, but employees can agree to work for longer than this. Any agreement to work longer hours should be made in writing, however. You can also average out the 48-hour week on an annual basis.

Employees are entitled to 4.8 weeks' paid leave each year. They are also entitled to other types of leave, such as maternity leave, paternity leave, adoption leave, parental leave (unpaid but within limits) and family leave (again, unpaid but within limits). Parents have the right to request flexible working if:

☐ they have a child under six years of age;

☐ they have a child under 18 years of age with disabilities; or

☐ they are the parent or carer of a dependent adult.

You have the legal responsibility to deduct tax and national insurance contributions from your employees' pay, but you cannot make any other deductions unless you are recovering an overpayment or have written permission from the employee so to do.

EMPLOYEE RIGHTS

Employees have rights other than those contained in their terms and conditions of employment:

☐ They have the right to the national minimum wage (see later in this chapter).

☐ There are regulations concerning minimum rest periods.

☐ You cannot take action that would undermine the trust and confidence your employees have in their relationship with you as an employer. Your employees, however, have an obligation to serve you honestly, faithfully and with care.

☐ You must provide your employees with a safe, secure and healthy working environment.

☐ Employees have the right to belong to a trade union.

☐ They are entitled to a reasonable degree of privacy and to protection against discrimination.

☐ They have the right to 'blow the whistle' on their employer's wrongdoings.

☐ Every employee is entitled to receive a payslip showing gross and net pay alongside deductions.

☐ Employees are entitled to a period of notice if they are employed for over one month, to keep their jobs during Transfer of Undertakings (Protection of Employment) Regulations (TUPE) changes (see below), and to a disciplinary and grievance procedure.

DISCRIMINATION AND EQUAL OPPORTUNITIES

It is illegal to treat employees less favourably on such grounds as race, sex, age, disability, pregnancy, sexual orientation, religion or marital status, etc. It is also illegal to treat someone less favourably because of their actions (for example, to victimize someone who has complained to their trade union about their employer's behaviour). You must take a share of the responsibility for any discrimination practised by your employees and you must investigate complaints thoroughly and impartially. Finally, you should not apply provisions or standards that a group or an individual is unlikely to be able to comply with. This could be viewed as indirect discrimination.

The main legislation on discrimination is contained in the Sex Discrimination Act 1975 and the Race Relations Act 1976. The Sex Discrimination Act and the Race Relations Act prevent unlawful discrimination on the grounds of sex, marriage and race in employment, education and training, the provision of goods and services and the disposal of premises. In addition, the Sex Discrimination (Gender Reassignment) Regulations 1999 make it unlawful to discriminate on the grounds of gender reassignment in employment and vocational training.

Similarly, the Disability Discrimination Act 1995 was designed to end discrimination against disabled people. It is a flexible piece of legislation that takes account of a business's individual circumstances. The main points of the Act are as follows:

- ☐ It aims to prevent disabled people from not having access to services or premises.

- ☐ Disabled people should not be treated unfavourably.

- ☐ Disability covers physical and mental impairments (including sensory impairments).

- ☐ It requires organizations to make reasonable adjustments to avoid 'substantial disadvantage' to disabled people.

- ☐ Landlords should not object to reasonable physical alterations to business premises to assist disabled staff and customers.

The Department of Work and Pensions suggests you should devise a 'better business checklist' to help you ensure you are meeting the requirements of the Act (see www.dwp.gov.uk). Although a great many of the provisions of this Act may seem irrelevant at this stage, when your business grows such information as that contained in the better business checklist will be essential for your continued expansion.

You should try to integrate equal opportunities into your business from the beginning. The first step to take is to devise an equal opportunities policy. This need not be long: a one-page policy statement that you can give to anyone who wishes to see it should be sufficient (Appendix III contains a brief equal opportunities policy you could adapt for your own business).

SICKNESS

You must pay statutory sickness pay (SSP) to qualifying employees for up to 28 weeks' sick leave. SSP should be paid from the fourth day of incapacity onwards. To qualify for SSP, employees must earn more than the lower earnings limit and must be aged between 16 and 65. In certain circumstances only can you end the employment of someone who has had repeat absences.

DISCIPLINARY ISSUES

You must have a disciplinary and grievance procedure, and this should be included in your employees' terms and conditions of employment. Your employees should be aware of what actions will incur disciplinary procedures. These procedures should follow the Advisory Conciliation and Arbitration Service (ACAS) code of practice (see www.acas.org.uk/index.aspx?articleid=1774).

Before you can dismiss an employee, you must demonstrate a good cause or reason: misconduct, illegal behaviour or incompetence, or an inability to do the job because of frequent and prolonged absences. Redundancy may also be grounds for dismissal, but redundancy is a carefully prescribed process that you should seek advice on.

You cannot dismiss someone for any of discriminatory reasons given above. Similarly, you cannot dismiss someone who reaches retirement age if they want to continue working. If you purposely make it difficult for someone to carry out their job, this may be construed as constructive dismissal, which is unfair. Employees who believe they have been constructively dismissed must first raise their grievance with you, and you will then have 28 days to reply. Should a subsequent employment tribunal uphold the employee's case, you could receive severe financial penalties.

Transfer of Undertakings (Protection of Employment) Regulations 2006 (TUPE)

At some point when running your business you will come up against the Transfer of Undertakings (Protection of Employment) Regulations 2006 (TUPE). The purpose of TUPE is to protect employees should the business they are working for change hands – for example, if you took on a new cleaning account and the cleaning staff were already in place. The TUPE regulations move the employees, and any liabilities associated with them, from the old to the new employer.

TUPE applies where there has been a 'relevant transfer'. To determine whether this has happened or not, the following factors are considered:

- ☐ The type of undertaking being transferred.

- ☐ Whether any tangible assets (buildings, moveable property, etc.) are being transferred.

- ☐ Whether any intangible assets are being transferred and their value.

- ☐ Whether the majority of the employees are being taken on by the new employer.

- ☐ Whether any customers are being transferred.

- ☐ The degree of similarity between the activities being carried out before and after the transfer.

- ☐ The period for which the activities were suspended, if any.

While you need not be fully conversant with every aspect of TUPE, it is important to understand how these regulations may affect you.

The TUPE regulations state that 'all the transferor's rights, powers, duties and liabilities under or in connection with the transferring employees' contracts of employment are transferred to the transferee'. Similarly, employees have the legal right to transfer to the new employer on their existing terms and conditions of employment and with all their existing employment rights and liabilities intact.

If you ignore the TUPE regulations, the employees have the right to bring a claim against you for unfair dismissal, redundancy, discrimination, unpaid wages, bonuses or holidays, and personal injury claims, etc. Any dismissals will be automatically unfair where the sole or principal reason for the dismissal was the transfer or a reason connected to the transfer. As noted above, you also cannot change the terms and conditions of employment of the transferred employees if the sole or principal reason is connected to the transfer.

CASE STUDY

X Ltd is unhappy with its current cleaning company. It has therefore invited companies, including yourself, to tender for the account. Your quote is successful and you take on the account. The previous cleaning company employed two members of staff. These people do not want to lose their jobs. The old company paid them £7.50 per hour, but your maximum hourly rate is £6.00. Under TUPE, you should not only continue to employ these members of staff but you should also match their current employment terms, including the hourly rate.

The question you may want to ask yourself is why this cleaning account was lost in the first place and, moreover, what part of this loss was down to the cleaning staff themselves. First, you should speak to the client about this. They may not be aware of TUPE and may have assumed that, by 'sacking' the cleaning company, they were also getting rid of the cleaning staff. They would probably say they want new cleaning staff when you take over – something, of course, you will feel obliged to provide. So, on one hand, you have an obligation to the client to provide the service they require. On the other hand, however, the law tells you that you must continue to employ the existing cleaning staff under the TUPE regulations.

The following are some steps you could take in these circumstances. First, inform the client of the TUPE regulations. Then suggest that the poor standards they experienced may not have been entirely the cleaning staff's fault. The previous cleaning company may not have:

☐ *trained the staff;*

☐ *invested time in managing them;*

☐ *applied quality control to the account, such as audits and follow-up; or*

☐ *motivated the cleaning staff or recognized their efforts.*

Next, advise the client you would like a period of time (say, a month or two) to work with the cleaning staff to give them a chance to improve themselves, thus complying with the TUPE regulations. Tell the client that, after this period of time, if there is no improvement in their standards, you will make an immediate change to the cleaning staff.

If you took this course of action you would be:

☐ *following the law;*

□ *keeping the client informed;*

□ *providing an opportunity to the cleaning staff to improve their standards; and*

□ *preparing to make the change, if required.*

To avoid paying the overly high hourly rates, there are two options:

□ *Inform all the parties of your hourly pay and seek confirmation in writing from the cleaning staff that they are happy to fall into this payment structure as part of the transfer.*

□ *Following the transfer, give the cleaning staff written notice that all staff must fall into your hourly pay structure. Provide them with the date of this change in their hourly rate.*

Either of these two steps could be argued against in a court of law and a decision taken against you. However, the parties involved in this type of situation are unlikely to take things to this level, and you exercised due diligence in your efforts to harmonize the transfer of the account with your company's structure.

When you find yourself in the situation of losing a cleaning account or selling your business, you must take the following steps to comply with TUPE:

□ You must inform and consult with the affected employees about the transfer and about any measures proposed.

□ Certain specified information must be provided to the employees long enough before the transfer to enable the employees to consult the outgoing employer about it.

□ If there are any changes or proposals for changes following the transfer, these must be discussed with the employees or their elected representatives.

□ If there is a failure to inform and consult, a complaint can be made to an employment tribunal. If successful, the tribunal can award whatever compensation it considers just and equitable, up to a maximum of 13 weeks' pay per affected employee.

You must also provide employee liability information to the new employer. You will have a duty to provide the incoming employer with written details of the transferring employees (including identity, age, particulars of employment, disciplinary and grievance records, employee claims and collective agreements), together with all the associated rights and liabilities that will transfer. This information must be passed not less than 14 days before the transfer, although in practice the incoming employer will ask for this information much earlier. If you fail to comply with this duty, the incoming employer can apply to a tribunal for compensation, which will be assessed with regard to the losses suffered with a minimum award of £500 per employee. A failure to comply with the TUPE regulations could therefore expose you to claims large enough to undermine the entire transaction.

There is no legal way to prevent TUPE applying to your business but, to lessen the negative effects, you should consider that any liabilities due are contractually shared by yourself and the transferring party. In all circumstances, it is recommended that you seek some specialist legal advice.

Applying the national minimum wage

The cleaning industry had always been notorious for low hourly rates, and so the national minimum wage has been beneficial to many cleaning staff. You will, from time to time, come across clients who show an interest in how much you pay your cleaning staff, so it is good policy to pay slightly over the minimum wage because this will reflect well on your business and can also be used as a selling tool: 'All our employees are paid over and above the national minimum wage.'

At the time of writing the national minimum wage is as follows:

- □ £5.52 per hour for workers aged 22 years and older.

- □ A development rate of £4.60 per hour for workers aged 18–21 inclusive.

- □ £3.40 per hour for all workers under the age of 18 who are no longer of compulsory school age.

It is a legal requirement that you pay your employees the appropriate rate of pay. This means that you will calculate your cleaning quotes based on the whatever the current national minimum wage is at the time.

CASE STUDY

❝ *In 1999 Mr Aslam quoted successfully for the X Ltd's cleaning account. The labour rate at the time was £3.70, so Mr Aslam quoted a rate of £5.45 per hour, which meant he was not only competitive but also profitable. He has consistently done a good job and so has retained the account.*

It doesn't take an economic genius to see that one of two things has happened:

Mr Aslam has never increased his charge to his client and is now paying £5.52 to his cleaning staff on an account that is only paying him £5.45 per hour – not to mention cleaning materials and so on.

Mr Aslam has increased his charge to his client proportionally each year and therefore remains profitable to this day. ❞

Every time there is a rise in the national minimum wage, therefore, you should increase proportionally your charges to your clients. There is a further benefit to this: you will increase your profits despite paying more to your cleaning staff. For example, you charge your client £410 per month for cleaning. Your labour costs are approximately £250. The minimum wage is about to increase by 7%. You notify your client 30 days before this increase that:

> ❝ *because your cleaning charges are calculated in line with the national minimum wage, and due to legislative increases in the direct cost of labour as a result of the national minimum wage, we will need to increase proportionally your invoice by the percentage increase in the minimum wage, which is 7%.* ❞

You then increase the £410 by 7% to £438.70. Your labour also increases by 7% from £250 to £267.50. You can now carry out a simple calculation:

□ Before the minimum wage you were charging £410. The labour costs were £250. The net difference was £160.

□ After the minimum wage you are charging £438.70. The labour costs are now £267.50. The net difference is now £171.20.

As you can see, because of the national minimum wage increase, you have managed to add an additional £11.20 per month to your cleaning account. If you do the maths you will see what this means on a turnover of £40,000 per month! The national minimum wage is therefore not only helping cleaning staff but it is also helping your profits. You will also find that few of your clients will dispute such an increase.

Control of Substances Hazardous to Health Regulations 2002 (COSHH) and colour coding

COSHH

Running a cleaning business means you will not be able to avoid the COSHH regulations. COSHH applies not only to cleaning but also to any industry that brings people and chemicals/substances into contact. Under the regulations, as an employer, you are required to:

□ assess the risks to health from chemicals and decide what controls are needed;

□ use those controls and to make sure your employees use them;

□ make sure the controls are working properly;

□ inform your employees about the risks to their health; and

□ train workers in the safe handling of such substances.

All the chemicals you use will have a COSHH safety data sheet. You should also be able to obtain such information from the manufacturer's website or by contacting the manufacturer directly. It is good practice to keep copies of all the relevant COSHH data sheets at each of your cleaning accounts.

The following is an eight-step guide to help you comply with the COSHH regulations:

□ **Step 1**: find out what hazardous substances are used in your work and assess the risks to people's health from using these.

□ **Step 2**: decide what precautions are needed before anyone starts to work with hazardous substances.

□ **Step 3**: prevent people from being exposed to hazardous substances. Where this is not reasonably practicable, control the exposure.

□ **Step 4**: make sure control measures are used and maintained properly and that safety procedures are followed.

□ **Step 5**: if required, monitor employees' exposure to hazardous substances.

□ **Step 6**: carry out health surveillance where your assessment has shown that this is necessary or where COSHH makes specific requirements.

□ **Step 7**: if required, prepare plans and procedures to deal with accidents, incidents and emergencies.

□ **Step 8**: make sure your employees are properly informed, trained and supervised.

You should carry out a risk assessment for each of your cleaning accounts, applying the above steps to help you identify the control measures that need to be taken to reduce and minimize the risks.

COLOUR CODING

You should know and remember the basic colour coding for cloths, mop heads and other cleaning equipment. This is essential both to maintaining hygiene and to avoiding cross-contamination.

It goes without saying that a cloth that cleaned the toilet bowl should not be used to clean kitchen work surfaces. Colour coding is the method applied to ensure this does not happen:

□ **Red**: sanitary appliances and washroom floors.

□ **Blue**: general and low-risk areas (apart from food areas).

□ **Green**: general food and bar-use areas.

□ **Yellow**: washbasins and other washroom surfaces.

□ **White**: disposables, such as those used in hospitals.

ASSESSING RISK AND METHOD STATEMENTS

With an ever-increasing awareness of the importance of health and safety in the workplace, more and more clients are now requesting a risk assessment and method statement for any outside contractor who works on their premises as a way of avoiding liability should something go wrong on their premises. While the onus is on you to present a risk assessment and method statement as you see fit, should a client ask for them, it is as well to remember that you will be held accountable if the procedures they contain are not followed. Apart from health and safety requirements, however, it will reflect well on your business if you can provide a risk assessment and method statement as standard.

There is no set way of presenting risk assessments and method statements: sometimes they may be supplied separately and, at other times, combined in one sheet. The example in Figure 13 applies to office cleaning. In this type of cleaning, the same risks tend to occur, and so it should be acceptable to create a generic risk assessment and method statement that will cover nearly all your clients' requirements.

If you are unsure about how to create risk assessments and method statements, there are many companies who can offer this service for you. However, you should really try to write your own because this will help you to understand them better should a client query any aspect of them.

Reporting of Injuries, Diseases and Dangerous Occurrences Regulations 1995 (RIDDOR)

The Reporting of Injuries, Diseases and Dangerous Occurrences Regulations 1995 (RIDDOR) place a legal duty on employers to report the following incidents to the relevant authorities by the quickest means possible:

☐ Work-related deaths.

☐ Major injuries.

☐ Over three days' injuries (where a person is away from work or unable to perform their normal work duties for more than three consecutive days).

☐ Injuries to members of the public or people not at work when they are taken from the scene of the accident to a hospital.

☐ Some work-related diseases.

☐ Dangerous occurrences (near miss accidents) – when something happens that does not result in an injury but could have done.

RIDDOR applies to all work activities, but not all incidents are reportable. If someone has an accident in a work situation where you are in charge and you are unsure whether to report it, you can call the RIDDOR Incident Contact Centre on 0845 300 99 23 for help and advice.

Method Statement

Company information	
Company details	The Cleaning Company Unit 10 Oak Tree Ind Estate Glasgow GXX 3XX Tel: 01234 567890
Site address	Your details
Activity – risk	To clean office premises safely

Implementation and Control of Risk	
Hazard Task – Risk	**Method of Control**
Cleaning windows (where appropriate)	Windows will be cleaned using appropriate ladders secured at bottom by second person
Removal of debris within building	Debris will be removed in appropriate refuse sacks with care taken not to overload sacks or persons
High-level cleaning	Cleaning at high level within building will be with use of appropriate step ladders and secured by second person where required
Wet mopping	Wet mopping will be appropriately signed and care taken by trained personnel
Vacuuming	All cables will be kept within office being cleaned and all machinery will be of safety-tested standard

Site control	
Customer awareness	The customer shall be kept aware of the progress of the work at all stages and immediately made aware of any problems or hazards that may occur

Fig. 13. Method statement for office cleaning

9

SALES, MARKETING AND ADVERTISING

Ninety percent of the success of any product or service is its promotion and marketing

(Mark Victor Hansen, motivational speaker)

Marketing and advertising should not be overlooked: you should constantly revise your marketing strategy to keep it fresh and noticeable. You should, however, obtain as much feedback as possible before you invest your money in marketing and advertising. While Coors probably did not intend to promote the joys and experience of diarrhoea, their slogan 'Turn it loose' translated into Spanish as 'Suffer from diarrhoea'.

Marketing and advertising

While marketing and advertising are often considered to be the same thing, they are, in fact, two entirely difference business practices. Marketing is the process by which your cleaning service is introduced to the marketplace. An advertisement is a description of your business that is intended to encourage people to contact you to take on your services.

Marketing is a time-consuming activity that involves a great deal of thought about how best to sell your services to your clients. Careful marketing should help to establish what type of company image would appeal most to your target clients. Marketing is, therefore, perception driven, and it will tell your clients:

□ whether you are a large or a small company;

□ whether you are a local or a national company;

□ whether your services are formal or informal; and

□ how professional you are.

Advertising is the implementation of this marketing. Before you spend money on elaborate advertising, however, you should first decide exactly who your target clients are. For office cleaning, for example, you should consider the following points:

□ In what location should I target offices?

□ Who is the correct person to contact?

□ How do I find out who this person is?

□ What type of advertising is likely to work for them?

☐ How will I know if they have received the information, and should I seek feedback?

This is the marketing process. You are thinking about how you are going to get from A to B in the quickest possible time and in the most cost-effective manner.

DECIDING THE LOCATION OF OFFICES TO TARGET

As a general rule you should target every possible location but, to begin with, you should try to identify areas where there are many offices: city centres, business parks, industrial estates, enterprise parks, science and technology parks and multi-occupancy buildings. Of all these areas and buildings, city centres are the most obvious to target because they contain a high number of offices.

CONTACTING THE APPROPRIATE PERSON

This can be a tricky: the person who deals with the cleaning is not always the decision-maker. Most of the time this person will only be putting together information to pass on to a manager or board, who will then assess this information and make the final decision. You will, in most cases, have no alternative but to deal with this nominated contact person. This person will more than likely be one of the following:

☐ the office manager;

☐ the office administrator;

☐ the office supervisor;

☐ the facilities manager; or

☐ the building manager.

FINDING OUT WHO THE CONTACT PERSON IS

Most businesses receive constant approaches from companies trying to sell them products or services. While some of these may be of value, most are not. Businesses in fact receive so much unsolicited information that most of it goes straight in the rubbish bin. To avoid this happening to your promotional material, take any or all of the following steps to identify who the contact person is:

☐ Call at the office and ask for the name of the person who deals with the cleaning.

☐ Email the office and ask the same question.

☐ Look on the company's website. This may provide contact details.

☐ Try Internet search engines, such as Google.

☐ Ask current or nearby clients if they know who the contact person is.

☐ Ask your cleaning staff if they can tell you who the contact people are in other cleaning jobs they may have.

If none of these work, you should at least address any mail to one of the five titles listed above.

SENDING THE CORRECT MESSAGE

What you send a potential client and how they react to it will determine whether your promotional material goes straight in the bin, into a file for future reference or results in the client phoning you. The following, therefore, are some tips for sending promotional material.

When posting, emailing or faxing, do not send:

- □ pages upon pages of information. This will look like a great deal of unnecessary reading the client could do without, and it will also block up their fax machine;

- □ anything handwritten – this will look really unprofessional;

- □ a dearth of information because this will have no enticement at all; or

- □ unnecessary pictures, animations or images in emails – keep it subtle.

You should simply send one of, or a combination of, the following:

- □ A one or two-page typed letter.

- □ A brochure.

- □ A glossy A4 information card.

- □ A personal yet professional message about you and your services.

- □ A well presented leaflet or flyer.

Use bullet points to highlight some of the benefits you can offer:

- □ Better prices.

- □ Better cleaning management.

- □ Cover cleaning staff always available.

- □ Regular audits.

Draw attention to any problems the client may be having with their current cleaning service and convince them that a change might be for the better.

CHECKING THE INFORMATION HAS BEEN RECEIVED AND SEEKING FEEDBACK

After 7 to 14 days, follow up the promotional material you have sent with a phone call. This will give you the opportunity to sell yourself further and to answer any questions the potential client may have. If they did not receive your promotional material, send it again. If you have emailed your promotional material, request a 'read receipt'. This will tell you that the person has received your email (see later in this chapter for more information on emailing).

You should create a database of the clients and companies you have contacted. This could be handwritten or kept on a computer. A database will help not only follow up but will also ensure you do not repeat advertise to the same client within too short a period.

Emailing

Emailing is now an essential business tool, and it is strongly recommended you use email if you are not already doing so. All professional companies with a sense of brand identity have both a domain name and a related website domain name. A domain name comprises the latter half of an email address (e.g. robert@thecleaningcompany.net) and the company's website address (e.g. www.thecleaningcompany.net). A domain name can be purchased for as little as £20, and you will have ownership of it for at least two years, with a renewal option at the end of this period.

The following are some of the ways emailing can benefit both the marketing and advertising of your business:

- ☐ Emails cost almost nothing to send.

- ☐ No paper is required, which is environmentally friendly.

- ☐ No postage stamps are required.

- ☐ There is no need to travel or to find a postbox.

- ☐ You can send the same information to many people using one email.

- ☐ You can receive replies almost instantly.

- ☐ You can track communications by date and time and can keep records.

Once you have established the name of the contact person at a company you wish to target, you have the raw ingredients of their direct email address. For example, the contact name is John Smith, and the company is XYZ Ltd. The email address for John Smith will be some configuration of JohnSmith@XYZLtd. This is, of course, not enough to construct a valid email address so, step by step, we must fill in the gaps.

First, what is the company's domain name? Answer: www.xyzltd.co.uk. We know that the domain name is made up of .co.uk (as opposed to .com or .biz, for example) and we also know that all the words in the domain name are joined together and in lower case. This now takes us a step closer to the completed email address: JohnSmith@xyzltd.co.uk.

Next, we need to find out how the first part of the address is configured – if this is not exactly correct, the email will not be received. There are many possibilities here (such as johnsmith, jsmith, js, smithj, etc.), so how do you find this out? You could do what most companies do and pay an information-providing company, such as Experian or Equifax, to supply this information. This would, however, cost somewhere in the region of £1,000 and may or may not be worthwhile. While you could also check business directory websites on the Internet, some of these may list the relevant contact people but most will not. The following method, however, is free and up to date. It may not always yield successful results but, given it is free, it is certainly worth a try.

Go to a search engine (Google is perhaps the best). Type in email @xyzltd.co.uk. The search engine should then produce a number of results linked to 'email' and the partial email address provided. When you go to the websites listed, the email addresses shown should be complete ones. From these you should be able to work out the first part of the email address. For example, let's say there are ten results with two complete email addresses: george.bush@xyzltd.co.uk and gordon.brown@xyzltd.co.uk. From this we can see that XYZ Ltd structures its employees' email addresses with forename and surname separated with a dot. It is a safe bet, therefore, that John Smith's email address is john.smith@xyzltd.co.uk.

This may seem like a convoluted process but it can be done in a very short period of time and it certainly beats paying for the information. The net result will be that your email will go directly the relevant person and, if the content of the email is both friendly and informative, you should receive a reply.

Once you have a list of email addresses, you have two options:

☐ The quick option – send one mass email to all the addresses on the list.

☐ The slow option – send an individual email to each person on the list.

The mass email option is the easier. You type all the email addresses into the 'BCC' section of the email you are about to send. You then send the email to yourself. This will mean that all the email addresses in the BCC section will receive an email, but they will not be aware it has been mass emailed to all the other people. With any luck, you should get a response from this. If you are unsure about how BCC works, simply type BCC into the Help option of the program you are using.

The slower option is more personal: you send an individual email to each email address and you will start each email with the person's name (e.g. 'Hi John'). You cannot apply this personal touch to mass emailing. The choice of which method to employ is ultimately up to you, but remember that the personal touch is the more effective.

The following are ten general tips to remember when emailing:

☐ Think before you write. Only send information that is relevant and useful.

☐ What you type is not the same as what you say. The written word is remembered long after the spoken word – and could be held against you!

☐ Keep your messages brief. Anything over one page should be sent as an attachment.

☐ The emails you send may not be treated confidentially – larger companies retain the right to check on their employees' emails.

☐ Be aware of how your email may be read by others – some words or expressions could be seen as argumentative, inflammatory or insulting even though this was not intended.

☐ Don't send repeat email after email – eventually they will be deleted even before they are read.

☐ Don't type all your emails in capital letters – this is the equivalent of shouting!

☐ Remember grammar. Just because it is email does not mean the rules of grammar do not apply.

☐ Try to be explanatory but concise in the 'Subject Line' – this is its whole point.

☐ Proofread before you hit the 'send' button – run the spellchecker to remove any grammatical or spelling errors.

Organizing stationery and promotional material

Anything that carries your company's name, services and contact details may be regarded as promotional material. If you have the budget, pay a printing company to produce your promotional material for you, but avoid ordering too much. Apart from the cost you will find that, as you grow, you may want to change your advertising, premises or telephone number. Of the 10,000 business cards you originally bought, 9,500 may now no longer carry up-to-date information.

Quality is important, so try to avoid:

☐ handwritten letters;

☐ homemade logos and letterheads;

☐ plain paper, single-colour leaflets;

☐ duplicate books for receipts or invoices; and

☐ Hotmail-type email accounts.

When designing your promotional material, try to incorporate the following factors:

☐ Information that will be relevant for as long as possible.

☐ A logo that is subtle, fresh and reflective of your company and industry.

- ☐ A basic, easy-to-read font – nothing odd or difficult to read.

- ☐ A clear and uncluttered presentation – think of the Google homepage (a basic but user-friendly interface).

- ☐ Bullet points for the services you offer.

- ☐ As much contact information as possible.

- ☐ Any awards you have or organizations you are accredited with (e.g. BICSc or the International Organization for Standardization).

The following are some of the basic stationery and promotional items you will require:

- ☐ **Business cards**: keep these simple (your logo, full contact details and a summary of the services offered). If you can afford it, have your business cards laminated, but in any event always choose good-quality paper.

- ☐ **Letterheads**: again, include your logo, full contact details and perhaps your slogan or a very few discrete words about your service. You may also want to include your VAT number, limited company registration number and any affiliations or memberships your company may have. Again, choose good-quality of paper.

- ☐ **Compliment slips**: these are handy to have. They should simply be a shorter and simplified version of your letterhead and can be used for any number of reasons.

- ☐ **Flyers or leaflets**: these normally have a short-term purpose – for a mailshot or a for a promotional drive for a discounted service or special offer. You will buy these in bulk fairly cheaply – but not too cheap! A5 is the generally accepted size.

- ☐ **Brochures**: these will be your most expensive stationery/promotional item. A wallet-type brochure is best that you can leave with potential clients or mail to the 'relevant' people. You can include further promotional material in these brochures (your business card, a letterhead, flyers, etc.). Get the design and content of these exactly right, and proofread them several times to avoid costly errors.

- ☐ **Website**: we look at websites in the next section of this chapter but, suffice it to say, you will want a basic website of some kind to start with.

- ☐ **Vehicle lettering**: whether you have a car or a van, you should have your logo and contact details on it. Also include your slogan or a short summary of your services. Screen printers have databases of all types of vehicle designs. Basic vehicle lettering can cost as little as £150 to £200.

Advertising on the Internet

The Internet has become an extremely important tool in getting information to consumers. The following are just a few of the benefits of Internet advertising:

☐ The Internet audience is unbelievably huge.

☐ You can target your advertising.

☐ You can track the success of your advertising.

☐ The entry cost for small-company advertising is low.

☐ The Internet is generally much cheaper than traditional advertising.

☐ The Internet has a greater range of possibilities than traditional advertising.

This section concentrates on three areas of Internet advertising: owning your own website, directory websites and search engine advertising.

OWNING YOUR OWN WEBSITE

Despite what some people may think, websites are not necessarily expensive. The cheapest are static, text-based websites. Next come flash websites (those that are entertaining – visual effects, animations, etc.). The most expensive are dynamic websites (interactive sites). Unless the consumables side of your business grows so large that you need online ordering and so on, it is unlikely you will require a dynamic website. Your choice, therefore, will be either a static or a flash website, both of which are fine.

If you are computer literate, you could try to build your own static website. This is a fairly simple process – all you need are the following:

☐ A domain name (see above).

☐ A program, such as Microsoft FrontPage, to design the site.

☐ Another program to upload it to the Internet, such as FTP explorer.

For anything more complicated than this, you should contact a website designer. Prices begin at a few hundred pounds, depending on the content you wish to include. Look at your competitors' websites to see how they present themselves. Whatever you include on your website, however, remember to keep it simple, informative and professional.

DIRECTORY WEBSITES

There is a plethora of business directories to choose from, some free, some that charge. Try to get into every free directory site you can and choose carefully from the ones that charge.

The most popular and widely used directory website is probably Yell.com. With Yell you have a variety of options:

☐ A free, basic listing.

☐ A paid-for listing.

- ☐ A paid-for listing with a link to your website.

- ☐ A sponsored listing (this is expensive but it will guarantee you are the first company listed in the chosen section).

- ☐ Additional listings for different sections (e.g. office cleaning, carpet cleaning, window cleaning).

The best advice is to call a sales representative who will inform you of the costs. You can then choose an entry level that suits your budget. You could also shop around – there are other sites, such as BT Business and Thomson Local. You might also choose to be in your local council or chamber of commerce directory. You may, however, have to be a paid member before your details go online.

SEARCH ENGINE ADVERTISING

Google has a very good advertising facility known as Ad-Words. With Ad-Words, you only pay when someone clicks on the advertising link to your website. If no one clicks, you pay nothing.

You can also set a limit on how much you want to spend each month. For example, when potential buyers type certain keywords into the search engine, such as 'office cleaning company London', your ad will display less frequently if your monthly limit is £50 rather than £100. It is, however, only when a potential buyer clicks on the link that you will be charged (the charge per click ranges from 30p to 90p). Bearing in mind the cost, the targeted nature of the advertising and the number of Internet users, you should consider using an online advertising tool such as this.

Networking

Networking is simply a way of putting yourself into situations, social or otherwise, where other business people meet. It is a great way to establish new relationships and to open new doors of opportunity for your cleaning business. While you don't need to be a flamboyant attention seeker to be an entrepreneurial networker, you should be prepared to sell yourself to some degree because, by selling yourself, you are selling what you represent – your fantastic cleaning company. Try to remember the following tips when in a networking situation:

- ☐ Be yourself – don't act in an unnatural way.

- ☐ Be open and willing to engage with other business people.

- ☐ Smile: people warm to smiles and shy from frowns.

- ☐ Engage in open-ended conversations – let people talk and listen to them.

- ☐ Focus on achieving something: have a purpose to your communications.

- ☐ Relax and enjoy networking – it's the light side of business.

☐ Make sure you have plenty of business cards on you.

☐ If it's a social event, avoid getting drunk (or too drunk!).

☐ Dress and present yourself well.

Business is all about relationships. If you can meet people and create the right first impression, you will be able to follow up on this and, potentially, develop a strong foundation for long-term and fruitful business dealings. Don't expect success to fall into your lap the first time of asking, however. Like anything else, your networking skills may need time to develop. The more you place yourself in networking environments the more familiar, settled and confident you will become in them.

To find out about local business networking evenings you should contact your local chamber of commerce. It will have a calendar for these events and will be able to give you advice on which ones may be suitable for you.

Making the most of opportunities

No matter how much networking you do, it will count as nothing if you don't recognize opportunities and reach out and seize them. As your entrepreneurial instincts develop, you will always be sniffing out opportunities for the greater good of your business. A good indicator of this is when your partner or spouse becomes embarrassed when you ask the waiter 'who carries out your daily cleaning service?' before dropping him a card.

You should also look for opportunities in your current cleaning accounts. For example:

☐ A cleaner is struggling to finish the job within the time allocated. Would the client agree to a longer period of time, thus increasing the charges and profit?

☐ A client's carpet is looking a bit dirty. You could measure up and drop in a quick carpet-cleaning quote.

☐ You are chatting with a client. Do they know another office manager they could recommend you to?

☐ You are chatting with a client. Do they have another office you could provide cleaning services for?

☐ A client's windows are looking dirty. Would they like you to organize the cleaning?

As well as looking for opportunities, you should perhaps be prepared to take a chance or two. Taking chances is one of the main differences between a standard business person and a successful entrepreneur. Taking chances is simply a measure of risk and reward: do the rewards of an endeavour outweigh the risks involved? Greater rewards bring greater risks, so how far are you willing to go to achieve your goals?

Don't stop pushing sales

From the day you start in business, bringing in new sales should never be far from your mind. In a competitive market such as cleaning, you will not build a decent-sized client base unless you constantly push sales using all the techniques discussed in this chapter.

Selling can be both demoralizing and highly fulfilling. When you become confident in the service you are selling, this will shine through when you are trying to win over a new client. When you get the job, there will be a terrific feeling of achievement. Give all the spare time you can to finding new clients and cleaning accounts:

☐ Send emails until your fingers and eyes are tired.

☐ Make telephone calls until the close of business.

☐ Scour the Internet for potential clients.

☐ Get out and about with leaflets and brochures.

☐ Constantly probe out new opportunities whenever you can.

If you build up and maintain momentum, by the law of averages you will succeed. Never let a week pass without having taken some positive steps towards creating new sales. In the early days, never let a *day* go past! The importance of dedicating your time to finding new sales cannot be emphasized enough.

10

MANAGING FINANCES

> *Diligence is the mother of good luck*

(Benjamin Franklin, scientist, inventor, statesman, printer, philosopher, musician and economist)

Managing finances is a crucial part of your business. You should try to develop a head for figures in order to manage your business properly, both on a day-to-day and long-term basis.

Creating business plans

A business plan allows you to put your ideas on paper so that you can start to allocate costs and draw together the information you require to set off on the right foot. If you intend to seek funding from your bank, a business plan is an essential requirement. It will help to prove that you have a well thought-out and winning formula to establish a cleaning business and, more importantly from the bank's point of view, that you will be able to pay back the money they lend you, interest and all!

The following are five important reasons for having a business plan.

FORECASTING YOUR DEVELOPMENT

This part of the plan looks at the goals aimed for, the resources required and the development expected – in other words, where you want to go and how you are going to get there. This will help you to understand the challenges ahead and to find success.

SECURING FUNDING

Whether for growth or investment, funding will be required at some point. To obtain funding and/or loans, you will be asked to provide not only accounts but also a relevant business plan. The accounts show the history of your business and the plan its future.

ESTABLISHING A COURSE OF ACTION

If you have identified opportunities for growth, set these out in your business plan as actions to take. You will then be able to measure your progress against your plan and revise it accordingly.

UNDERSTANDING AND MANAGING YOUR FINANCES

In the early stages, your business plan will help you to maintain profitability and, at the very least, to break even. It will help you to manage your finances and to avoid insolvency. Further, it will help you to plan for the future: if you manage your cash flow well, you should accumulate reserves for future investment.

CONSIDERING A POTENTIAL EXIT STRATEGY

It may be your intention to set up and run a cleaning business for five years and then to sell the business after this period. To obtain the best possible return, it is important to have a well thought-out business plan that will be attractive to potential purchasers.

You can design your own business plan, find a free business plan template on the Internet or seek professional advice and assistance. Whichever method you choose, try to avoid making the following mistakes:

- □ **Poor quality**: if your plan has been put together hastily and is ill-presented in terms of both grammar and content, it will achieve little.

- □ **Watch the numbers**: anyone casting a professional eye over your business plan will be looking to assess the validity of the numbers. Wild projections, incorrect calculations and unrealistic cash-flow forecasts will not stand up to scrutiny.

- □ **No opportunity shown**: avoid complicated and long-winded technical plans with over-complicated formulas and/or charts. The people who will look at the plan will consider only that information that tells them exactly what the opportunity is.

- □ **No clear direction**: your plan must show how you intend to penetrate the cleaning industry and how you will grow. The 'idea' of a cleaning business is not enough to secure funding – you should show how this idea will become a practical success.

- □ **Over-optimism**: temper your plan with a degree of realism. It is unlikely you will become the country's market leader in contract cleaning within one or two years, so bear this in mind when you illustrate how many clients you expect to accrue.

- □ **Poor cash-flow understanding**: your understanding of cash flow should be sound. You may be profitable but you do business on credit terms so, if the money does not come in quickly enough to pay the bills, you may soon become insolvent – a very common occurrence in business.

- □ **Lack of demand**: consider what demand there is for your service. If you live in a sleepy rural backwater, there may not be enough demand for your service.

Raising capital

You may need to raise capital to cover part of your salary, to purchase equipment and/or a vehicle or to invest in advertising. If you borrow, borrow an amount that gives you a financial cushion: borrowing the least amount required leaves no room for the unpredictable. Similarly, do not over-borrow. While you should ensure you have a safety net, remember that you will have to pay the loan back – with interest.

One of the main problems in raising capital is that you may not have a proven track record. To overcome this, you should be positive and confident and should support your request for a loan with a strong, solid business plan. If you are seeking funding from an individual financier or a family member or friend, you should use this relationship to your benefit. Seek to involve this person in your ideas: court their advice and encourage them to see your vision. Once they 'see' the idea, they should be more forthcoming. Don't let the fact your company is small stand against you: stress the fact that, being a small company, your clients receive a much more personal and professionally managed service than those provided by larger companies.

Consider the following points when attempting to raise capital:

☐ As noted above, encourage potential financiers to buy into your idea – people take more interest in something they have contributed to.

☐ Understand your business plan – be ready to explain its content and demonstrate you know how to manage your cash flow.

☐ Know your competitors. Be prepared to explain how your service is better than your competitors' and how this will ultimately mean more business for you and less for them.

☐ Be ready to answer any questions your business plan may throw up. If you are truly prepared the answers will come naturally. If not, your business plan may lose plausibility.

☐ Don't be afraid to play on the abilities and qualities you have that cannot be measured by a business plan or balance sheet: you may have proven skills in an industry other than cleaning. These same skills could apply to your new cleaning business. Use everything you have at your disposal to increase your chances of funding.

Choosing a bank

It is often not the best decision to stick with the bank that holds your personal current account: business banking is extremely competitive, so shop around and compare the products and services that are on offer. Also remember that you are not committed to a bank for life. Changing banks after your business is well established, however, is an onerous task, so take your time and choose wisely.

The following are some of the things to look out for when choosing a bank:

☐ If you are a sole trader you can use your personal account for business banking. If you are a limited company, however, you must open a business account. It is recommended, however, that you open a business account whatever type of company you form because a business account is a better way to track your finances.

☐ Choose a bank that supplies business support – a bank that will offer you a business manager or business team.

☐ Bank charges can soon add up, so try to compare the fixed charges for such things as cheques, BACS payments and overdrafts.

☐ Look out for offers for new business account customers, such as reduced or free charges and other incentives.

☐ Find out what else the bank can offer you in terms of credit card deals, overdraft facilities, etc.

☐ Compare the interest rates for business accounts. As your money grows, you may want to move to a high-interest account.

☐ Find out if there are free Internet banking services.

Once you have chosen a bank you may be asked to provide certain information in order to open an account:

☐ If a limited company, a certificate of incorporation.

☐ Various identifying documents (utility bills, a passport, etc.).

☐ A list of signatories who can sign cheques.

☐ A completed mandate (provided by the bank).

☐ A copy of the partnership agreement, if applicable.

☐ Any property agreements, leases or freeholds related to your business.

ONLINE BANKING

Online banking saves time and allows you to pay your bills, to set up direct debits and, most importantly, to operate your payroll efficiently and effectively. A business online banking program is, in fact, essential from a payroll point of view. For example, in a year or two you might be employing forty or more part-time cleaning staff whom you pay on a fortnightly basis. It will be impractical, if not impossible, for each person to receive a cheque or cash on pay day. With online banking you can make all your payments on your PC at a time suitable to you. In order to do this, you should have a process in place to bring in all your cleaning staff account details within the fortnightly payroll system.

With online banking you have the choice of paying your staff by BACS or CHAPS. CHAPS is the better because it is a same-day transfer, but CHAPS costs more than ten times as much as BACS. BACS operates on a two to three-day transfer period, so the payments you put through during business hours on a Wednesday will arrive in your employee's account on a Friday. There is also an option to schedule payments in advance, if this would suit your payroll system better.

Some online bank accounts, particularly the free ones, set limits on the amount of money you may transfer in one working day. These limits vary, but £10,000 is about average. When your business grows, therefore, you may need to upgrade to a paid online banking service.

CREDIT CARDS

Sometimes you may need to buy cleaning materials, equipment or uniforms from a company with which you do not have a credit account. Credit cards are useful on such occasions because they give you a period of credit. Pay your credit card bill by direct debit to make sure it is settled every month. After a while you may want to increase your credit card limit to give yourself greater flexibility in managing your finances and making purchases. Finally, take all possible measures to protect yourself from credit card theft and fraud (for example, as soon as your credit card arrives, sign it, and cut old credit cards into small pieces, etc.).

Managing your overheads

Overheads are the operational costs of running your business (for example, accountancy fees, advertising costs and depreciation). Because overheads do not yield any direct profits, how you manage them will have a direct bearing on how profitable you are. You should, therefore, monitor your overhead costs and continuously look for ways to reduce them. For example, you may be renting an office that is more expensive than it needs to be, your telephone bills are too high or your supplier's prices are not as competitive as they could be. Don't simply accept your current overheads as set in stone: it is down to you to reduce them and to increase profit margins accordingly.

Buying machinery

Because this book mainly discusses daily cleaning and office cleaning, this section concentrates on the machinery required for these types of cleaning: basic vacuums, wet vacs, scrubber dryers and rotary buffing machines.

BASIC VACUUMS

Your most expensive piece of frequently used machinery will most likely be a general vacuum cleaner. While other machinery may be more expensive than a vacuum, a vacuum will be necessary for almost every cleaning account and will probably be used on a daily basis. As mentioned earlier in this book, for small cleaning accounts it is better if the client supplies the vacuum because such accounts are not very profitable and the cost of a new vacuum will eat into what profits there are.

There are three types of general vacuum cleaner: tub vacs, back vacs and upright vacs.

Tub vacs

The well-known Henry Hoover is the classic 'cleaner's tub vac' and is used widely throughout the industry. It is not the only tub vac and is not necessarily the best, but it is moderately priced, robust and synonymous with daily cleaning. While it is the obvious choice, there is nothing to stop you from shopping around for a different brand if you would prefer something else.

Henry has a number of brothers: James, Charles and Edward, to name but a few. Recently there has been a female addition to the family – the pink Hetty Hoover. If you choose the

Numatic range of Henry vacs, tell your cleaning staff to avoid the following actions because these can result in faults and breakdowns:

☐ Tugging the hose and handle tubes when the wire is at full stretch because this will damage or loosen the internal connection.

☐ Using their feet to switch the vacuum cleaner on and off, thus damaging the switch mechanism.

☐ Bumping the vacuum cleaner down the stairs, which will damage the wheels and internal parts.

☐ Bending the hose at the handle connection too much because this will eventually cause it to split.

☐ Twisting the tube connection into the floor tool, which will damage the connection.

☐ Vacuuming up too many large objects, thus blocking the floor tools, tubes or hose.

☐ Using the vacuum cleaner without a bag (which is very common) because dirt and dust will get into the motor, causing it to break.

Keep the boxes and instructions for all your vacs so that you can troubleshoot faults or, if they are still in their warranty period, return them to the supplier or manufacturer.

Back vacs
Back vacs have many advantages but, unfortunately, they have disadvantages as well. Nilfisk sells the Backuum, which is much like a rucksack. Straps go over each of your shoulders and the machine is strapped to your back like a scuba diver's tank.

Back vacs have the following advantages. They are:

☐ ergonomically designed;

☐ very flexible and mobile;

☐ professional looking compared with a Henry Hoover;

☐ easy to use; and

☐ adjustable for different body shapes.

They also have the following disadvantages:

☐ They are expensive, as are spare parts.

☐ Cleaners often feel embarrassed when wearing them.

☐ It is difficult to move quickly between vacuuming jobs because you have to take them off and then put them back on again.

☐ They can become warm, which may irritate your back if you wear them for a long period of time.

Upright vacs

Most people in the cleaning industry will say that a good upright vacuum is the best choice for quality vacuuming. The main reasons for this are that commercial upright vacuums are solid, professional looking, easy to use and, importantly, have rotary brushes as well as good suction. Rotary brushes will lift the general, day-to-day soiling a carpet will receive. Numatic and Henry tub vacuums have rotary brush attachments, one of which is rotated with air, the other being powered.

Commercial upright vacuums, however, cost almost twice as much as a Henry Hoover and around the same as a Backuum. The best advice, therefore, is to start with the Numatic range and to invest in one or two upright vacuums as your business grows (whether you buy back vacs is up to you!). See SEBO's website (www.sebo.co.uk/) for a range of commercial upright vacuums.

WET VACS

Once your business expands, it is wise to invest in a wet vac (Numatic and many other suppliers sell these, so shop around). Wet vacs come in a variety of sizes, but a medium-sized one is perhaps best to start with.

A wet vac is very handy for:

☐ one-off cleans;

☐ builders' cleans;

☐ floor deep cleans;

☐ soaking up leaks and small floods;

☐ any mopping tasks that require a quick uplift of water or a fast dry time; and

☐ floor strips and seals.

SCRUBBER DRYERS

As you would expect, scrubber dryers scrub floors clean and also dry at the same time. A good scrubber dryer will cost over £1,000, so you may initially want to buy one second hand or perhaps hire one as needed: like wet vacs, you will not use a scrubber dryer very often unless you have taken on an account that specifically requests the regular use of one. In such circumstances you should build the purchase or lease cost into the quote for the job.

Scrubber dryers are either mains or battery powered, and they come in various sizes, from the smallest all the way to ride-on size. If you acquire big cleaning accounts, such as large stores, shopping centres or airports, scrubber dryers will be a necessity.

ROTARY BUFFING MACHINES

You should invest in at least one buffing machine because many accounts will require them and because they have a number of uses. Buffing machines come in a variety of sizes and speeds. Typical sizes are 13, 15 and 17 inches, and speeds range from approximately 150 rpm (slow) to 300 rpm (high speed).

What you use the machine for will dictate its size and speed. For example:

- □ **Buffing a polished floor daily to a high shine**: a 17-inch, high-speed 300 rpm machine.

- □ **Scrubbing a wet floor to clean it**: a 15-inch, slow-speed 150 rpm machine. If there is water and dirt on the floor, a high-speed machine will simply splash this all over the walls as it spins. A slow-speed machine with a smaller disk will ensure a more manageable clean.

- □ **Shampoo brushing a carpet**: a 13-inch, medium-speed 230 rpm machine. A small machine is easier to manoeuvre around obstructions, and a medium speed will ensure a good clean without damaging the carpet.

To begin with, a medium-sized, medium-speed (15 inches, 230 rpm) machine should do for most circumstances. There are also various accessories and attachments that can be used with these machines, some of which are essential, some not:

- □ Drive board: attaches to the bottom of the machine. Used for attaching buffing pads to.

- □ Coloured buffing pads: *white* – for a dry polish and high-shine finish; *red* – for wet polishing and light scrubbing; *blue* – for wet, medium-duty scrubbing (abrasive); and *black* – for deep scrubbing, stripping polish and heavy soiling (very abrasive). There are other coloured pads, but these are the most popular.

- □ Bristled brush attachments.

- □ Nylon shampoo, scrubbing, polishing and stripping brushes (these come in various standards to suit the job in hand).

- □ Solution tank: a handy accessory for carpet cleaning, wet scrubbing and related tasks. There is a trigger handle to release the tank solution at floor level.

- □ Bonnet mops: various types of waxing, polishing and buffing attachments that also come in microfibre. They are good for carpet cleaning.

Organizing materials and supplies

While it may be tempting in the start-up period to nip down to your local supermarket to buy a few tins of the supermarket's own-brand polish or a cheap bowl cleaner, this will not reflect well on your business should your client look in the cleaning cupboard. You should, therefore, choose a commercial cleaning range and buy in bulk, keeping all the COSHH data sheets (see Chapter 8) in a safe and accessible place.

You should control the costs of the chemicals and materials you use. Unfortunately, your cleaning staff may not share your enthusiasm for cost-cutting, so do not provide them with unlimited supplies – they will soon disappear, along with a percentage of your profits. The following are some tips to help avoid this:

- ☐ Do not hold stock at your cleaning accounts because it will be used more quickly than if stored elsewhere.

- ☐ Don't use cheap J-cloths if you can avoid it – they will be used once and then thrown away.

- ☐ Don't allow your cleaning staff to use blue roll/centre pull as a cleaning cloth because this is not reusable.

- ☐ Keep records of deliveries so that you can measure the frequency of use per account.

- ☐ Don't be afraid to challenge your cleaners about the amount of materials being used – using more is not necessarily best practice.

- ☐ Don't replace such things as buckets if all they need is a good clean.

- ☐ Always try to repair a vacuum cleaner before replacing it.

- ☐ Only deliver what the cleaners need or ask for.

- ☐ If the client makes available cleaning materials or chemicals, encourage your cleaners to use them.

- ☐ Try to buy 5-litre bottles with pump-action, refillable heads as opposed to 500 or 750-ml trigger sprays. These are more cost effective and will last longer. Similarly, tell your cleaners not to throw away any empty trigger-spray bottles because these can be reused with 5-litre refills.

- ☐ Encourage the use of microfibre cloths. These are expensive but are very effective and are reusable for up to three months if maintained properly. Educate your staff in how to use them correctly. Likewise, ask your cleaners to take cloths and mop heads home to wash them. If they won't, do this yourself.

While some of these points may seem extremely miserly, remember that, the less you spend on unnecessary supplies, the more profit you will make.

❮ *The following cleaning materials and supplies are likely to be required for an office cleaning account where one cleaner works for two or three hours per day:*

☐ *A vacuum cleaner: most offices will require a vacuum.*

☐ *Mop buckets: blue and red if there are toilets to be cleaned and possibly green if there is a kitchen.*

☐ *Mop poles: as above, colour coded to the bucket.*

☐ *Mop heads: again, as above. Supply two of each initially.*

☐ *Cloths and dusters: a range of colour-coded, good-quality cloths, including dishcloths, microfibre cloths and possibly scrim for glass cleaning. Also, lint-free dusters.*

☐ *A flick duster: for high-level dusting.*

☐ *A soft brush and shovel: for general sweeping and the collection of floor debris and rubbish.*

☐ *Phone wipes: not simply wipes but disinfecting, anti-bacterial cleaners.*

☐ *A glass cleaner: choose a good glass cleaner – some are poor.*

☐ *A multi-surface cleaner: a good, general-purpose cleaner.*

☐ *A kitchen cleaner: an anti-bacterial surface cleaner for food preparation areas.*

☐ *A washroom cleaner: a disinfecting cleaner for washroom surfaces.*

☐ *A bowl cleaner: for inside toilet bowls and urinals.*

☐ *An air freshener: a general item that may come in handy.*

☐ *Polish: for real wood and other areas that require polish. Modern office environments, however, do not require much polish. Most modern office furniture has a coated veneer finish, so there is no 'wood' to polish. It is a popular misconception among cleaning staff that all surfaces should be polished. This is not the case: a damp, clean, microfibre cloth will do a good job and can be reused over and over again.* ❯

Bookkeeping

Bookkeeping is the recording of all the financial transactions you undertake in the running of your business. It can be performed using pen and paper but, with the growing complexity of tax regulations and to minimize errors, accounting software is increasing being used.

BOOKKEEPING METHODS

There are a number of different ways to record the day-to-day financial transactions of your business: bookkeeping books, spreadsheets, accounting software programs or employing a bookkeeper.

USING BOOKKEEPING BOOKS

The simplest and most cost-effective way of bookkeeping is to record your transactions manually on paper. You could use plain paper with headings for all your transactions or you could buy an accounting book (such as a Simplex D) that has a page for each week of the year for recording your income and expenditure, weekly bank reports and creditors.

Even though this method is easy, it is tedious and fraught with error. Once your business grows, you will require another method. To record your transactions manually, however, you will need to log the following information:

- **Income**: date, reference, description, amount, payment method, where you allocated the income to (e.g. bank or petty cash).

- **Expenses**: date, reference, description, amount, how you paid it, expense heading (e.g. stock, fuel, phone charge, rent, materials, etc.).

USING SPREADSHEETS

There are various spreadsheet programs you could use, or you could simply opt for Microsoft Excel. The following are some advantages of using spreadsheets:

- Unlike paper, you can correct mistakes easily and can add new columns.

- You do not need to use a calculator – at the click of a button your spreadsheet program will do the calculation for you.

- You can save time by copying and pasting information as and when required.

- You have all the benefits of a computer program: automatic totalling if you change the numbers, spell checking and printing/saving/emailing, etc.

While spreadsheet programs are an extremely useful tool, they are, however, limited in comparison with full accounting software programs.

USING AN ACCOUNTING SOFTWARE PROGRAM

Before we look at the two main programs available on the market, it is worth noting that your bank may provide you with free business-planning or management software. While perhaps not as comprehensive or as user friendly as the two commercial programs, this software may, at least, be worth looking at. NatWest, for example, offers a free program that includes 'Things to think about before you start' (a series of checklists and guides), a business planner and 12 months' free use of MyBusiness Essentials software, etc. Before you buy a commercial software package, therefore, you could check what your own bank supplies with its free software.

The two main commercial programs are Sage and Quickbooks. You should be able to buy this software at a level that suits your business, and they are both user friendly and fairly easy to understand. They offer vast amounts of reports that should help you to understand your business and to identify areas of both strength and weakness. They also do all your tax and percentage calculations for you and track information on outstanding payments and when invoices are due for payment.

While the Sage software is the software your accountant will be familiar with and is the software your clients are also likely to use (which makes the cross-checking and corroborating of reports easier when chasing debts, for example), there is, however, one major area where Quickbooks is the better option.

In time you hope to be employing a great many people, most of whom will be part time and who will work for a few hours a week only. The Sage software does not take into account the number of part-time staff a business has when categorizing it as small or large. A cleaning business that has forty employees, of whom only two or three are full time, is, therefore, treated as a 'big' or 'bigger' business. As a result, for this business you would have to buy a more expensive add-on program than Quickbooks in order to obtain updated tax tables, certain payroll-tracking features and other, related information.

EMPLOYING A BOOKKEEPER

While employing a bookkeeper is an excellent way to record your business transactions, a bookkeeper will not only cost you a great deal of money but will also deny you an extremely important opportunity to learn how a business is run. Try not, therefore, to take this option because it is vital that you develop an understanding of bookkeeping as both a business person and an entrepreneur. That said, it would, of course, be foolish to rule out a bookkeeper completely: simply consider your own circumstances.

Choosing an accountant

Of all the advisers you will encounter, a good accountant is perhaps the most valuable. If your accounts are in order and you are up to date with your payments, you are more likely to be able to concentrate on building your business. The following, therefore, are ten tips on choosing an accountant, as suggested by the small business portal, Bytestart (www.bytestart.co.uk/):

☐ Investigate and, if possible, choose an accountant before you start your business.

☐ Make sure your accountant is fully qualified (for example, as a certified or chartered accountant). These qualifications will probably be displayed on promotional material or on the company's website. If not, make sure you ask.

☐ It is essential that your accountant works with small business clients. If your business generates a large number of transactions (for example, an online shopping service), make sure the accountant has experience of dealing with companies in your sector.

☐ How much does the accountant charge? Is there a fixed annual or monthly fee to complete all business tax requirements, or do hourly fees apply? Compare the fees of several firms.

☐ When you first meet a prospective accountant, you will know soon enough whether you see eye to eye. It is important to develop a good relationship and to know that your finances are being handled by someone you can trust. You should contact at least three accountants and find out which one best meets your requirements.

☐ What other services does the accountant provide? Can they complete your self-assessment returns? Do they provide business advice or further information to help your business grow?

☐ Because you are a small business, the best accountant for you is also likely to be small. A small accountant will understand what it's like running a small operation and will have the resources and time you require to manage your finances properly.

☐ Ask to speak to existing clients before signing up. A decent accountancy firm should be happy to arrange this.

☐ Make sure your accountant keeps in touch with your business – not just at the year end! If you feel your current accountant no longer meets your requirements for whatever reason, get a new one.

☐ If at some stage you decide to sell your business, you will need a good accountant more than ever to minimize any tax liabilities payable on the sale.

Arranging insurance

Businesses that employ staff and that operate in public areas will almost certainly require business insurance. The minimum insurance you will typically require are public and products' liability insurance and employers' liability insurance. These can usually be provided in one combined policy, and there are also some additions you can make to the policy specifically related to contract cleaning. For example, optional cover for:

☐ fidelity (dishonest employees);

☐ financial loss;

☐ lock and key replacement;

☐ fines (such as for rubbish left out in non-council bins); and

☐ the misuse of clients' telephones.

Your insurance cover will be assessed by the number of employees you have and/or by the level of your turnover, the latter option generally being the better. At the start your insurance will not be too expensive but, as you grow, so will the cost of your insurance.

The following is a summary of the different types of business insurance and what they are for.

LEGAL LIABILITY INSURANCE

Public liability

This insurance protects you against claims from third parties because of injury (or death) or harm done to property as a result of any of your business activities. This type of insurance is unlikely to apply to, say, a web-design company, but would be necessary if members of the public had access to your business premises (e.g. a shop or service centre).

Employers' liability

This type of insurance protects your business against claims from employees, including claims for accidents and sickness.

Professional indemnity

This insurance covers you if you act in a professional capacity during the course of your business. In some types of work, such as accountancy, professional indemnity insurance is a legal requirement.

Directors

Even though the limited nature of a limited company 'limits' claims against its directors, in some cases (e.g. negligence) the directors of limited companies may be sued. This type of insurance protects directors from this.

OTHER TYPES OF BUSINESS INSURANCE

Equipment

This type of insurance covers all your business equipment, subject to the terms of the policy.

Buildings and contents

This is standard insurance that covers your business property and fixtures/fittings. If you are working from home, contact your household insurer to make sure your policy extends to your home business needs.

Motor

Again, this is standard insurance for business transport. If you use your own vehicle to run your business, make sure your insurer is updated in the change in your circumstances.

Legal expenses

This covers you in the event of legal action being taken against your business, including court costs and legal fees.

Cushions and cautions

It is perhaps fitting to end of this chapter with a word of caution. If you work hard, you should enjoy the fruits of your labour but, like my father advised me: 'Cushions and Cautions!' Just because there is money in the bank does not mean it is there to be spent frivolously.

You should keep financial 'cushions' of capital available at all times to counter the unexpected or to get you through tough times. Likewise, you should practise 'caution' when spending your hard-earned money and should always seek to minimize your overheads and to avoid risky investments.

11

TAX AND NATIONAL INSURANCE

I told the Inland Revenue I didn't owe them a penny because I lived by the seaside

(Ken Dodd, British comedian and singer-songwriter)

While a great deal of the information contained in this chapter about tax and national insurance is available from the Inland Revenue, it is summarized here in the light of running a cleaning business.

Registering for Value Added Tax (VAT)

VAT is a tax that applies to most business transactions that involve the transfer of goods or services. Once your turnover reaches a certain level, you will have to register for VAT. This means that, whenever you buy or sell something in the course of your cleaning business, you will have to charge VAT on your sales, keep proper VAT records on your incoming and outgoing transactions and pay VAT to HM Revenue & Customs (HMRC).

If you are registered for VAT, you will pay VAT on purchases (input tax) and charge VAT on sales (output tax). If you charge more output tax than you pay in input tax, you must pay the difference to HMRC. If, on the other hand, you pay more input tax than you charge output tax, HMRC will refund the difference.

At the time of writing, you must register for VAT if you supply taxable goods and services with a total value of more than £64,000 in a 12-month period or if you anticipate supplying taxable goods and services valued at more than £64,000 in the next 30-day period alone. Certain types of goods and services, however, are not taxable and are therefore exempt from VAT (e.g. insurance, loans and some types of education and training).

There are three rates of VAT: standard (17.5%), for most goods and services, including cleaning; reduced (5%), for such things as domestic fuel and power; and zero (0%) for food, books and newspapers, etc. You pay VAT on a quarterly basis. At the end of each quarter, HMRC will send you a VAT return. You record in this the amount of VAT payable and how you have calculated this. Your completed VAT return and your payment are normally due one month after the end of your tax quarter.

You may find that, as your cleaning business grows and you become VAT registered, you lose some of your domestic clients for whom you do carpet or general cleaning. These clients may want to swap to non-VAT registered businesses, thus saving themselves 17.5% of the cost.

National insurance

Most people in work have to pay national insurance contributions (NICs) as well as tax. NICs are collected by HMRC. There are three different levels of NICs: earnings threshold (ET), lower earnings limit (LEL) and upper earnings limit (UEL). There are also different types of NICs. The following are the ones you are most likely to encounter:

☐ **Class 1 primary contributions** (paid by employees earning over the ET): employees pay Class 1 NICs at a one percentage rate on their gross earnings above the ET up to and including the UEL and at a reduced percentage rate for earnings over the UEL. These NICs are deducted at source from the employees' salaries.

☐ **Class 1 secondary contributions** (paid by employers on the salaries of those of their employees who earn above the ET): employers pay Class 1 NICs on their employees' gross earnings over the ET at a single percentage rate. There is no UEL for employers' NICs. These are usually paid to HMRC on a monthly basis, together with the employees' primary NICs.

☐ **Class 1A contributions** (paid by employers): payable by employers on their employees' benefits in kind, such as a company car or private medical insurance. These are calculated and paid annually.

☐ **Class 1B contributions** (paid by employers): payable only by employers who have entered into a PAYE (Pay As You Earn) settlement agreement with HMRC to account for tax on certain expense payments and benefits.

☐ **Class 2 contributions** (paid by the self-employed): payable by the majority of self-employed individuals at a flat rate, either monthly or quarterly.

☐ **Class 4 contributions** (paid by the self-employed): payable by self-employed individuals who have made a certain amount of profit in a year. Calculated annually using the self-assessment tax return form.

Deducting tax and managing the payroll

PAYE (Pay As You Earn) is HMRC's system for collecting income tax from the pay of employees – including directors – as they earn it. As an employer, you must deduct income tax and NICs from your employees' pay (including any directors) before they receive it and submit the deductions to HMRC. When you calculate these deductions, you must also take into account the various rates, allowances and limits that exist.

You must send the most recent amounts you have deducted from all your employees' pay to HMRC by the 19th of each month (or, if you make electronic payments, by the 22nd of each month). If you pay too little or too late, you may incur interest on these amounts or a fine.

PAYE applies to *all* money you pay your employees, or the cash equivalent if you provide shares or vouchers, for example. These payments include the following:

- ☐ Salary.

- ☐ Overtime and/or shift pay.

- ☐ Expense allowances and claims.

- ☐ Bonuses and commission.

- ☐ Statutory sick pay.

- ☐ Statutory maternity/paternity/adoption pay.

- ☐ Lump sum payments, such as redundancy.

FORMS

There are four main forms you will have to deal with regarding your cleaning staff:

- ☐ **Wage slips**: you are obliged to provide a wage slip to show your employees what they have been paid and what has been deducted from their wages.

- ☐ **P45s**: new employees will provide you a P45 stating their tax code and year-to-date totals. Likewise, you will provide a P45 to any employee who leaves your employment.

- ☐ **P46s**: because of the high turnover of cleaning staff, you will find that a great many new employees will not have a P45. You must therefore get these new staff to complete a P46. These can be obtained by calling the Employers' Order Line (see Appendix I).

- ☐ **P60s**: these are given to your employees at the end of the tax year. They show their total deductions for the whole tax year.

Corporation tax

If your cleaning business is a limited company, you will be liable for corporation tax. Your accountant will usually calculate once a year how much corporation tax is due, but you still have a legal responsibility to maintain records of your business transactions. These transactions include the following:

- ☐ Details of all receipts and expenses incurred in the course of your company's activities.

- ☐ Details of all sales and purchases made in the course of trade, if your company has a trade that involves dealing in goods.

- ☐ All other supporting documents.

Your corporation tax return must be sent in within a certain time frame or you will incur penalties. Payment of the tax itself is due exactly nine months and one day after your normal due date. For most companies, the normal due date is the last day of the accounting period. So if a company's corporation tax return covers the accounting period 1 January 2009 to 31 December 2009, then the corporation tax should be paid no later than 1 October 2009.

Income tax

Each year you will be required to complete and return a self-assessment tax form. Self-assessment returns are issued in April each year and cover the year from the previous 6 April to the current 5 April. For example, the 2008–9 tax year covers the period from 6 April 2008 to 5 April 2009.

You will normally receive a tax return through the post. However, you are legally responsible to make sure you have one if this does not happen. To start with, you will receive the basic self-assessment form (SA100), which contains a great deal of information applicable to everyone. Further to this, you will require supplementary pages that are based on your legal entity. The most common supplementary pages are as follows:

- **Employment** (SA101): if you are an employee or company director.

- **Self-employment** (SA103): if you are a sole trader.

- **Partnership** (SA104): if you are self-employed in a partnership.

If you fill in your return on paper and you want HMRC to work out how much tax you owe, you must send it back to HMRC by 30 September. If you send it back later than this, you will have to do your own calculations. If you choose to complete and file your return online, however, the system will work out and immediately show you how much tax you owe or are owed. In any case, your return must reach HMRC by 31 January. If you miss this deadline, you will be liable to an automatic penalty of £100. You may also be charged additional penalties and interest on any overdue tax payments.

Do not worry overly about completing these forms – your accountant should be able to assist you, if required. They seem very long but are actually quite straightforward, once you understand which sections apply to you. If you do your best to keep good payroll and deduction records, this will help you enormously.

Claiming capital allowances

As a business, you can claim tax allowances – called capital allowances – on certain purchases and investments. This means you can deduct a proportion of these costs from your taxable profits and thus reduce your tax bill. The amount of the allowance depends on what you're claiming for.

The Inland Revenue (see Appendix I) can supply you with more information on the following capital allowances and related topics:

- Capital allowance on plant and machinery.

- Capital allowance on buildings.

- Working out your capital allowance claim.

☐ Claiming capital allowance.

☐ First-year allowances.

Working out your business expenses

Whichever way you set up your cleaning business, whether it is a limited company, a partnership or sole trader, you must consider which business expenses are allowable and should be reported.

Your business expenses will fall into one of two categories for the purposes of self-assessment: allowable and non-allowable. Broadly speaking, you can deduct from your turnover all the costs you incur for the sole purpose of earning business profits. These are known as allowable expenses. The following are some examples of the types of cost that are allowable as legitimate types of business expense:

☐ Goods purchased for resale.

☐ Materials used by the business to make goods to sell.

☐ The rental of business premises.

☐ Electricity for heating, lighting and manufacture.

If you claim for vehicle expenses, you must remember that, if the vehicle is also used for private use, only the business proportion of the use counts as an allowable expense. For example, if your total vehicle expenses were £3,000 and one third of your mileage was private, only two thirds of the cost can be claimed against tax. In other words, if the total cost of your vehicle expenses is £3,000 but private mileage makes up £1,000, only £2,000 can be claimed against tax.

12

CONTROLLING DEBT

Debt has become a part of who we are

(Dave Ramsay, money expert)

When you first start in business, debt may seem a distant problem, but it is something you should always keep an eye on. Debt can build up quickly, and you should be prepared to chase a debt the moment the agreed credit period expires. This chapter, therefore, looks in detail at debt management.

Managing credit

There is a difference between credit management and debt management: when a client fails to pay their bill, this is debt management; credit management involves devising a system whereby you receive revenue from your business in the timeliest manner possible.

From the very beginning you should establish and continuously monitor an effective way of managing credit. If you manage credit well, you should reduce the amount of debt management you need to undertake. The following are some tips about credit management from the finance managers, Insight Associates (www.insight associates.co.uk/):

CASH IS KING

C – customize: prevention is better than cure. Payment terms must be clear from the outset.

A – analyse: identify your best customers and set credit limits.

S – systemize: rapid invoicing is a must.

H – harmonize: do your homework.

I – incentivize: positive motivation for payment can produce results.

S – socialize: don't be shy – talk and communicate with your customers.

K – kryptonize: don't let your money vanish into thin air – keep it safe.

I – itemize: state the facts clearly and concisely.

N – neutralize: make safe – don't lose more than you need to.

G – generalize: when is a sale not a sale?

While we may be unsure about what is meant by 'kryptonize', these are all good tips.

Credit is a fact of the business world, and you will generally provide your clients with standard, 30-day credit terms. These standard terms are widely used by, and are expected from, nearly all cleaning companies: very few clients will pay up front. The whole point of credit terms is to permit the natural ebb and flow of business finances, thus providing clients with a breathing space while they wait for a return in revenue from their business activities.

When your clients are experiencing negative economic conditions, however, this may have a negative effect on your own business. Good credit management should help to reduce these effects.

An unfortunate consequence of being a young and growing company is that you cannot pick and choose your clients. You may, therefore, be more susceptible to bad debts. Consider what the large, national cleaning companies do to avoid debts:

☐ They acquire, and hold on to, good clients.

☐ They can, to a certain extent, choose their debtors.

☐ They have effective methods for sifting out potentially bad clients.

☐ They almost always check their clients' credit ratings.

☐ They often employ full-time staff to deal with debtors.

☐ For these reasons, consistently bad debtors do not contact large companies – they contact you! The sooner you implement a professional credit management procedure, therefore, the sooner your company will move forward.

Establishing your invoice dates

A common mistake is to wait until the end of the cleaning month before sending out the invoice for that month. For example, cleaning begins on 1 January and, on 31 January, you send out your invoice for the January clean. The 30-day credit terms mean an end-of-February payment. Clients can and do, however, take up to 60 days to pay, and so you may not receive payment for January until the end of March. You pay your cleaning staff fortnightly. This means you will pay staff at least six or seven payments before the end of March. You have, therefore, paid a great many of the wages out of your own pocket, having had no return from your client.

This is not an ideal situation. While you will always be behind slightly because your cleaning staff are paid fortnightly, to pay three months' worth of wages out of your own pocket is not good business practice. There are, however, ways to overcome this problem.

First, you could consider paying your staff on a monthly basis. While some cleaning companies operate this policy, it is generally disliked by cleaning staff and could be a deciding factor in whether or not you recruit good cleaning staff. Secondly, you could invoice for your cleaning services in advance. This would mean sending your invoice at the beginning of January on 30-day terms, with payment due at the end of January.

Some clients may question this, but stick to your guns – such a policy will help greatly with your cash flow. Simply explain to your clients that they have indeed received an invoice early but that they should not worry about paying it straightaway: it is on 30-day terms and, because your cleaning becomes chargeable from the first day of the month, it is for this reason you have instigated start-of-the-month invoicing. Few will argue with this.

Issuing statements

You should send your clients monthly statements. These should contain information about the last few invoices and will thus draw your client's attention to their growing level of debt. Statements should include the following:

☐ Invoice numbers and their dates.

☐ The total value of each outstanding invoice.

☐ If possible, a short description of what the invoice is for.

☐ When each invoice was due for payment.

☐ A list of any recent payments made.

☐ The total outstanding money due, broken down into 30, 60 and 90-day, etc., periods.

Clients make all sorts of excuses for not paying invoices on time (they had a query on it they were going to ask you about when you chased them for payment, they 'never received it', etc.). By issuing statements you are not only drawing your client's attention to what money is outstanding but you are also showing them that you are fully aware of this money and that you are in the early stages of pursuing it.

Pursuing debt

Once a debt exceeds the normal 30-day business terms, you should set in motion procedures to recover it. When an outstanding invoice becomes a bad debt – that is, a debt of over 60 days – you should do all you can to achieve the best financial outcome for your business. First, try to keep the lines of communication open. Do not fall out with your client or upset them because, if you do and they really are in trouble, you will be the last creditor to be paid. By simply talking to your client you may find out why they cannot pay, and you may be able to work out an agreeable solution. This solution, however, must suit you, not your client.

Many of your clients may have to wait a very long time to be paid themselves and, while you may appreciate their situation, this does not mean they should neglect to pay you on time. If there is a pecking order for prompt payment, you may find you are low on it and that those creditors who are paid on time are the ones who escalate their demands for payment by using a solicitor or debt collection agency. If you suspect that others are being paid before you, go to the next stage of formal debt recovery: employ a debt collection agency yourself.

Most debt collection agencies will not charge if they do not recover a fee so, if it looks as though you are unlikely to receive an outstanding payment, you have nothing to lose in employing a debt collection agency. Debt collection agencies generally charge a percentage of the debt collected and, the higher the debt, the less they will deduct as a collection fee. For example:

Debt = £10,000; collection fee = 7.5%
Debt = £1,000; collection fee = 10%

The first thing a debt collection agency will do is send a signal that you are serious about collecting the debt. They normally begin with frequent telephone calls to pursue the debt. If this does not yield results, the next stage is to issue a statutory demand for payment.

A statutory demand gives your client 21 days to pay the debt. After this period has expired and the debt has still not been paid, a bankruptcy or winding-up petition may be issued. Most creditors regard a statutory demand as the legal equivalent of a 'warning shot from a gun': the average debtor is so scared of what may follow that they usually pay up. For this reason, statutory demands are successful in 99% of cases. A debtor may, however, dispute the claim for payment, in which case the statutory demand will be set aside. Should the case subsequently go to court and the court decides against the claim, an order for costs may be made on the creditor.

The statutory demand procedure is simple to implement:

☐ To issue a statutory demand, all you need to do is complete a form.

☐ You can send a statutory demand by recorded post. You do not need to deliver it personally.

☐ You do not need a solicitor to issue a statutory demand.

☐ You do not need to pay expensive court-filing fees.

Most people assume that a solicitor has been employed to issue a statutory demand and so pay up immediately. Some companies, however – particularly those that are consistently bad debtors – know that a statutory demand is a bluff technique. If a statutory demand does not work, therefore, and depending on the level of debt owed, you may need to go further to receive payment.

Winding-up and bankruptcy petitions

Winding-up and bankruptcy petitions are also ways of trying to recover your money. Unpaid tax and wages, however, will take priority over other debts for any funds available.

Winding-up applies to companies rather than to individuals. After the winding-up, the company will cease to exist. If the company was insolvent, not all the creditors will be paid in full, and each creditor will therefore receive a percentage of what they are owed.

Bankruptcy applies to people or general partnerships. If a general partnership, all the partners are made bankrupt. The assets are sold and the proceeds are paid to the creditors. Each creditor will again receive a percentage of what they are owed.

Factoring

Factoring is the process of releasing up to 85% of the value of your invoices as soon as they are issued, which allows you to put the money to work where it is needed most. If your cash flow dictates that you must be paid within a 30-day period in order to maintain your working capital, then you could consider factoring. Factoring, however, incurs costs: only if you really need the capital and cannot wait the standard period of time is factoring worth considering.

The first step is to ask for quotes for factoring services. Costs and services vary considerably, however, so you should seek impartial advice, if possible, before you buy a factoring service. The factoring fee comprises two parts:

☐ A service fee covering the day-to-day servicing of your purchase ledger, which is usually between 0.5 and 3.0% of your turnover.

☐ An interest charge, which is charged against the amount of each invoice. This is usually a fixed percentage above the factor's base rate.

Factoring companies can also manage your invoices and the collection of unpaid debts. Such companies suggest that this will give you more time to develop your business, using the working capital from your outstanding invoices.

Although the management of invoices and the collection of unpaid debts are an integral part of factoring, you do not need to make use of these services to release cash from your invoices. If you use a factoring company solely to release cash from your invoices, this is known as invoice discounting. As with factoring, invoice discounting can release up to 85% of the value of your invoices almost as soon as they have been issued, but invoice discounting, unlike factoring, allows you to retain control of the management of your invoices and the collection of your unpaid debts. Because of this, invoice discounting is typically aimed at large organizations that have the staff and resources to manage their invoices and unpaid debts.

13

MANAGING YOUR EXPANSION

Ever since I was a child I have had this instinctive urge for expansion and growth. To me, the function and duty of a quality human being is the sincere and honest development of one's potential

(Bruce Lee, movie star and martial artist)

You should consider the expansion of your company carefully: what may work for a small cleaning company may not work for a large one, and there are constant challenges to be faced as your business changes and grows.

Coping with the problems of growth

While expanding your company should include expanding your profits, with growth come the inevitable growing pains: you will find that expansion brings problems that can only be met by reinvesting these profits.

It is a common belief among business people that you can rarely find staff who will treat your business and clients the way you do – no one is willing to put in the hours you do or to go that extra mile for your clients. If you do find someone who meets your expectations, you must reward their application because good management staff can sometimes be harder to find than good cleaning staff.

Quality supervisory or management staff are essential if the following growth problems are to be avoided:

- ☐ Your clients do not receive visits and your cleaners are not checked regularly.

- ☐ Standards are rarely checked and, when they are, no follow-up takes place.

- ☐ Cleaning shifts are missed and cleaning staff receive no support.

- ☐ Payroll errors occur frequently.

- ☐ Client complaints are not dealt with.

This list could go on. The fact is, you cannot do everything yourself.

Recruiting service managers

The term 'service manager' is used here. The following terms, however, are also employed to describe the senior members of the cleaning/operational staff:

☐ supervisors;

☐ account managers; and

☐ operations managers.

The person who assumes this role will take over or share the day-to-day duties you will eventually grow out of as you concentrate your efforts on your company's development.

The main duties of a service manager are as follows:

☐ Covering cleaning accounts when there are short-term absences or arranging suitable cover.

☐ Advertising locally for cleaning staff.

☐ Organizing and delivering cleaning materials.

☐ Meeting and inducting new staff.

☐ Client liaison.

☐ Audits, detail lists and follow-ups.

☐ Supervising one-off cleans, such as builders' cleans.

☐ Payroll recording.

☐ Reporting back to you daily on such things as a member of the cleaning staff leaving, a new one starting, if a client has complained, if the cleaning hours have been changed and so on.

The obvious course of action is to employ a member of your cleaning staff whom you believe could fulfil this role. To begin with, you should employ someone on a part-time basis, with overtime for any additional work required. You will know when the time is right to take on management staff, but the following may give you a guide:

☐ Turnover reaches £15,000–£20,000 per month – part-time manager required.

☐ Turnover reaches £25,000–£30,000 per month – full-time manager required.

☐ Turnover reaches £40,000–£50,000 per month – two full-time managers required.

When your turnover exceeds £60,000 per month, this is the time to consider an operations manager. This person will manage not only the service managers but also the clients, who will be seeing less of their service managers as the accounts build and their roles become purely operational.

For both part and full-time positions, you should look for the following qualities in the candidates:

- ☐ **Hard working**: covering cleaning shifts and working long hours mean you must employ someone who is a natural hard worker.

- ☐ **Presentable**: this person will have to deal with clients and will therefore need to dress and present themselves accordingly.

- ☐ **Flexible**: early starts, late finishes and plenty of short-notice absences dictate that this person must be able to 'drop and go' as the business requires it.

- ☐ **Leadership skills**: this person must be recognized by the cleaning staff as an authority figure.

- ☐ **Conscientious**: this person must do what is right and must make the right choice, not the easy one.

- ☐ **Reliable**: cleaning accounts can be 7 days a week, 365 days a year. This person must be reliable.

- ☐ **A good driver**: cleaning accounts are often widespread, so this person must be a good driver.

A full-time service manager will have to work flexible hours and so should be on a salary as opposed to being paid hourly. Because cleaning work is mainly done early in the mornings and late in the evenings, a full-time service manager should work a split-shift system (for example, 7 a.m. to 1 p.m. followed by 4 p.m. to 7 p.m.). This will enable you to cover the core operating hours without making someone work a 12-hour day. The service manager should organize their off time around these hours: they must be prepared to put the company's needs first.

A full-time service manager will require a mobile phone and a small company vehicle.

MOBILE PHONES

You should choose a monthly contract option using the same network as your own mobile phone. This will help to reduce the costs of the extra mobile phone. A call package of around £35 per month, including text messages and free call time, should suffice.

Make sure you are sent itemized bills, and check these for calls made late in the evening or at weekends. If there are a great many calls during these times, ask your service manager about them. If they are not business related, claim the cost of these calls back, but it does no harm to allow a small tolerance of a few pounds each month as a gesture of goodwill. You should, however, emphasize the fact that the mobile phone is strictly for business use, unless otherwise agreed. You could have this written into your service manager's contract of employment.

COMPANY VEHICLES

Because of the hours involved, it is not practical to provide a company vehicle during working hours only. The only solution, therefore, is to let your service manager have the vehicle all week. You will, of course, be concerned that the vehicle is not used for shopping trips or for collecting children from school. You should, therefore, monitor the vehicle's use.

The most effective way to do this is to install a software-based tracking device in the vehicle. Tracking devices cost around £30–£40 per month per vehicle, and you may be required to commit yourself to, at the very least, a three-year contract. Tracking devices, however, are an excellent way of keeping tabs on your service manager, and they will provide you with the following information:

- ☐ What time the vehicle was started in the morning.

- ☐ Where the vehicle went.

- ☐ What time it stopped and for how long it stopped.

- ☐ Where it went next.

- ☐ How many miles where covered, and so on.

You can set the tracking device to email you a report every morning of the previous 24 hours' vehicle movement, with all the above information included. It can also provide 'real time' information on the vehicle's location: you simply logon to the service and it will show you on a map where the vehicle is. (See www.minorplanet.com for a company that provides such a service.)

Employing administrative staff

While a service manager will help you with the operational side of your business, administrative staff will help you with the day-to-day administration of your business. When you decide to employ an administrative assistant, look for someone with experience of the cleaning industry who also has a strong, office-based background. Initially, employ this person on a part-time basis – when you are confident that your business is growing and that there are sufficient profits to do so, you might then decide to pay this person a salary.

The key roles for an administrative assistant are as follows:

- ☐ Answering the telephone and dealing with the mail.

- ☐ Sending out invoices and chasing payments.

- ☐ Dealing with client queries.

- ☐ Advertising jobs, managing your cleaners' database and undertaking some marketing duties.

- ☐ Sharing some of your service manager's duties.

- ☐ Assembling client welcome packs.

☐ Maintaining payroll and general records, such as employee contracts.

☐ Organizing health and safety information, such as COSHH.

☐ Ordering cleaning materials and general stationery and assisting in the general running of your business.

Managing the payroll

As your business grows, several things will complicate your payroll recording system:

☐ Absences, overtime and additional shifts.

☐ Different rates of pay for different jobs.

☐ New staff starting and old staff leaving.

If you employ upwards of 50 cleaning staff, it is very easy to miss not only an extra shift here and there but also a member of staff altogether!

To avoid this, on one sheet, record the following information:

☐ The account name.

☐ The number of cleaners per account.

☐ The number of hours per clean.

☐ The number of cleans per week.

☐ The total cleaning hours for the fortnightly pay period.

Such a system should prevent you paying a cleaner 2 hours for a 1.5-hour clean. You could then use this master sheet each fortnight to cross-check with your daily payroll records. These daily records should capture the information listed above – namely:

☐ Absences, overtime and additional shifts.

☐ The different rates of pay for different jobs.

☐ Whether any new staff have started and whether any staff have left.

Cross-check this information with your master sheet. The total fortnightly hours per cleaner should match the total hours on the master sheet. When the totals do not match, you should investigate this to make sure no member of staff is being paid too little or, worse, too much! When everything is correct, the information from your final payroll sheet should be entered into your accounts so that the necessary deductions can be made to arrive at the net amount payable.

Pay close attention to your payroll recording. When you do go wrong the member of staff concerned will be quick to complain and will expect immediate action. This could involve an extra trip to the bank and then a trip to the member of staff, as well as an amendment to your accounts.

The following are some tips on how to organize your fortnightly payroll. If you pay your staff fortnightly (every second Friday, for example), you can do this in one of three ways. Paid up to:

☐ the payment day (no arrears);

☐ the previous Friday (one week in arrears); or

☐ two Fridays ago (two weeks in arrears).

PAID UP TO THE PAYMENT DAY (NO ARREARS)

This may be the most suitable way to organize your payroll when you first set up your business:

☐ **Advantages**: you will attract more cleaning staff because they are paid for the fortnight they have just worked.

☐ **Disadvantages**: if you pay by BACS, you will need to make the payment on the Wednesday before the Friday payday in order for it to clear in time. You will, therefore, need to estimate what your cleaning staff will be doing on the Thursday and Friday, and you could end up making an overpayment if your staff leave your employment on one of those two days or are absent.

PAID UP TO THE PREVIOUS FRIDAY (ONE WEEK IN ARREARS)

Of the three choices, this is probably the most suitable:

☐ **Advantages**: you have a period of time from the end of payroll period (Friday) until the following Wednesday to calculate your staff's wages for a two-week period that has already passed.

☐ **Disadvantages**: if you start with the first system and then change to this (or even the next) system, you will upset your staff because they will have to wait longer to be paid.

PAID UP TO TWO FRIDAYS AGO (TWO WEEKS IN ARREARS)

This option is, again, better for you but worse for your staff:

☐ **Advantages**: this system will give you an even longer period of time in which to calculate your payroll.

☐ **Disadvantages**: cleaning staff will choose a job that pays by the first or second methods before they would choose one that pays this way because they will have to wait for up to four weeks to receive their first pay packet.

Retaining your clients

As noted on many occasions in this book, one of the key reasons for your success will be the fact that you have been dealing with your clients personally and have therefore been supplying a high level of service. As you expand, however, you will find that you have less daily contact with your clients, and this may in time lead to retention problems if the staff you employ to look after your clients are not meeting the minimum standards your clients have come to expect from your company.

While large cleaning companies accept a certain level of churn in their cleaning accounts – simply adding new accounts when they lose old ones – retention is extremely important for success. Poor retention means that any new accounts that are added are simply replacing ones lost, with the result that you are merely treading water, not growing.

The following, therefore, are ten tips on retention from Allbusiness.com (www.allbusiness.com/):

☐ **Market to your existing clients**: your current customers are already doing business with you and are more likely to buy from you again. Focus most of your time, efforts, and resources on better serving your current clients. Go deeper instead of wider.

☐ **Be consistent in your approach and interactions**: treat your clients with honesty, humour and respect – and maintain this over time. If you are consistent with them over time, they will see you as dependable, credible and trustworthy.

☐ **Follow through on your commitments**: if you promise to send information or to follow up, do it. You will gain loyalty and trust by always doing what you say you will do.

☐ **Connect with your customers**: find out about their lives, their hopes, goals and desired outcomes. Ask questions that encourage a deeper sense of shared understanding. The greater the level of connection, the greater the mutual satisfaction.

☐ **Have fun**: it's easy to get caught up in goals, outcomes and deliverables. Of course these are important, but clients also want to work with people who enjoy what they do. The more fun you can have while providing strong outcomes, the longer your clients will stay.

☐ **Position yourself as a resource for life**: let your customers know you will be around for a long time. Let them know they can get back to you whenever they need you. This can help to differentiate your company from your competitors, who may just be in it for the short term.

☐ **Ask for feedback and input**: at some point in the working relationship, solicit feedback. Ask your clients how they feel about working with you and ask if they have suggestions for how the working relationship or outcomes could be improved. Asking for their ideas shows that you care about their opinions and value their contributions.

☐ **Share resources**: do you know of a good book your clients might benefit from reading? Tell them about it. Do you have the name of someone who could help a client move ahead on their business plan? Tell them about it. Sharing resources is a terrific way to build loyalty and satisfaction.

☐ **Reward them for staying with you**: consider implementing a loyalty scheme where your long-term clients are rewarded for staying with you. You might offer them gifts, products or services for a certain level of ongoing participation with your business.

☐ **Keep learning**: the more you focus on gaining new knowledge, skills and experiences, the more you have to offer your clients. The more you have to offer, the more they will benefit. The more they benefit, the longer they stay. Keep focused on your own professional growth and learning. Both you and your clients will benefit.

14

PROPERTY SERVICES

❝ Opportunities multiply as they are seized ❞

(Sun Tzu, author and military strategist)

This chapter looks at the opportunities beyond cleaning. If you have the ability and desire to diversify your services, this chapter should give you some food for thought about how you can improve your profit margins using the same clients but different services.

A lucrative add-on

You are always very efficient in the provision of your cleaning services, so what is to stop you from being very efficient in the provision of other services? The office managers you deal with have, for example, the responsibility not only for organizing a cleaning company but also for the general maintenance services required for the smooth running of a busy office. So what is stopping you from providing these services as well? To provide a cleaning service, you do not need to be a cleaner yourself. Similarly, to provide an electrical service you do not need to be an electrician. When you deliver multiple services to your clients you will find you are:

- ☐ tapping into much greater profit margins;

- ☐ receiving additional work and income;

- ☐ expanding your knowledge and abilities outside cleaning;

- ☐ securing your position with your clients, particularly with cleaning provision;

- ☐ building a foundation for new and exciting growth areas; and

- ☐ assisting your clients with their jobs, which they will be very grateful for.

As mentioned on several occasions in this book, it is very easy to criticize cleaning, but few people who work in offices have a wide-ranging knowledge of such trades as plumbing and electrical work. Because of this they are not as quick to judge plumbing or electrical work unless, of course, a job has obviously been done badly.

Most of your clients will have experienced difficulties in finding good and reliable tradespeople (not showing up as agreed, not returning to a job after starting it, poor-quality work, etc.). Such problems cause anxiety and, even though a client may use one company for all their servicing requirements, they may still experience difficulties. The next section, therefore, looks at the various add-ons you can offer your clients that will not only provide them with a better service but will also yield high profits.

Offering additional services

As you develop this side of your business, you should try to provide the following services:

- □ General reactive and planned maintenance services.

- □ Electrical and plumbing services.

- □ Flooring, partition wall and suspended ceiling services.

- □ Portable appliance testing.

- □ Small building and civil work.

- □ Refurbishment work.

- □ Blacksmith and welding services.

- □ Roofing maintenance and repairs.

- □ Painting and decorating.

This may seem like a big list but, once you have found the right subcontractors, you will find it is not difficult to manage. (We look at subcontractors in detail in Chapter 15.)

GENERAL REACTIVE AND PLANNED MAINTENANCE SERVICES

General reactive and planned maintenance services cover the following basic areas:

- □ Light bulb 'lamp' changes.

- □ Minor repairs, such as faulty door handles, loose toilet seats, etc.

- □ Minor electrical work, such as cracked sockets, etc.

- □ Moving furniture.

- □ Mounting shelves and whiteboards to walls and so on.

- □ Transporting items locally.

- □ All typical 'handyman'-type jobs.

In sum, this is a handyman service delivered professionally. You should offer this service (and all your services) reactively – on a two to four-hour response basis. Your clients will be delighted by this response.

For cleaning provision you will charge £8.50–£9.50 per hour. For general maintenance work, you can charge anything from £15 to £20 per hour, but you need to pay your directly employed general maintenance staff only marginally more than the minimum wage.

You will be surprised how many companies will sign up for this service. Large offices, in particular, have a regular need for some type of maintenance work, as do business centres with their high turnover of office space because of short-term lets.

ELECTRICAL AND PLUMBING SERVICES

Electrical services

Electrical services cover many areas but, in general, most jobs involve electrical maintenance work or minor installations, such as the following:

☐ Lighting faults.

☐ Light fittings, switches or sockets that are buzzing or faulty.

☐ New or additional sockets.

☐ Moving electrical floor-boxes.

☐ Adding new lights or replacing old ones.

☐ Repairing or replacing kitchen or toilet extractor fans.

☐ Replacing faulty fuses or circuit breakers.

☐ Tests and inspections related to British Standards 7671.

Most of this work can be undertaken by any qualified electrician. If, however, larger-scale work is needed, ask your electrician for advice so that you can price the work accurately.

Plumbing services

Nearly all that has been said about electrical work applies to plumbing services. Plumbing maintenance and minor installation work includes the following:

☐ Toilets leaking or not flushing.

☐ Replacing toilets.

☐ Repairing leaking pipe joints.

☐ Replacing sinks and faulty taps.

☐ Unblocking toilets and sinks.

☐ Replacing faulty water heaters.

☐ Repairing waste pipes.

☐ Stopping water-tank overflows.

FLOORING, PARTITION WALL AND SUSPENDED CEILING SERVICES

FLOORING SERVICES

The type of floors you will deal with include carpet tiles, sheet carpet, vinyl, Altro, Polyflor, various hardwoods and laminate, etc. Your general maintenance person may be capable of looking after carpet tiles, sheet carpet and perhaps even basic vinyl. For other types of flooring you will have to employ a qualified contractor, particularly for commercial vinyl, which requires an experienced fitter for screeding, hot-welding joints and so on.

Partition wall and suspended ceiling services

Both these services involve a wide range of installations, such as partitions, metal and timber stud, all glass, plasterboard ceilings, ceiling tiles with a suspended grid and ceiling tiles with a fixed grid, etc. With the correct training these are not difficult tasks and, more importantly, they are very profitable.

PORTABLE APPLIANCE TESTING

Portable appliance testing is commonly know as PAT testing but, formally, it is called the 'in-service inspection and testing of electrical equipment'. There is a misconception that PAT testing can only be carried out by qualified electricians. This is not strictly true, but it does require a basic understanding of how insulation and earthing work, etc. PAT testing is usually conducted on an annual basis, so it is a good way of building up a fair amount of repeat business.

Local companies often offer one-day training courses in PAT testing. You would receive a certificate for attending such a course, and the cost may be anything from £250 to £350 per person. If you undertake the course yourself, you will be able to earn up to £40 per hour for testing appliances.

A good-quality PAT testing machine costs about £1,000. You will need to buy labels to attach to appliances, and you will provide your clients with reports and certificates at the end of the testing. These are retained by the client to prove they are observing health and safety regulations. If companies do not have their appliances tested, this may invalidate their insurance.

SMALL BUILDING AND CIVIL WORK

Small building and civil work includes the following:

☐ Minor road and car park repairs.

☐ Building or repairing walls.

☐ Installing posts (such as car park signs).

☐ Supplying and installing fences.

☐ Plastering and wet-trades work.

☐ Roughcasting, mono-blocking and so on.

These services are not required on a regular basis but, if you have taken on a new client who is looking for a 'one-stop shop' for all their property needs, you should try to provide these services.

REFURBISHMENT WORK

When individual jobs, such as painting and laying carpet tiles, are combined, this can be considered as refurbishment work. There are a great many opportunities for this type of work, which is discussed in more detail at the end of this chapter.

BLACKSMITH AND WELDING SERVICES

There is a surprising amount of blacksmith and welding services work:

☐ Installing, repairing or replacing handrails, fences and spindles.

☐ General steelwork repairs to locks, doors and hinges, etc.

☐ Installing and repairing gates, mesh fences and enclosures.

ROOFING MAINTENANCE AND REPAIRS

In bad weather, the need for a roofer may be both sudden and urgent and, when a roofing repair is urgent or is an insurance claim, the price will be higher than for a routine repair job. The problem for you in such circumstances may be that, if you are not employing a roofer directly, the one you contract to do your work is snowed under with calls themselves from their own clients. The result may be, therefore, that you cannot provide a reactive service that will reflect well on you.

Roofing maintenance and repairs work includes the following:

☐ Replacing missing or broken tiles.

☐ Unblocking or replacing gutters.

☐ Repairing leaking roof lights.

☐ Repairing cladding sheets or lead flashing that leaks or is damaged.

☐ Clearing flat-roof puddles and repairing leaks at the seams.

☐ Moss and gutter clearance.

☐ Corrugated-roof repairs.

PAINTING AND DECORATING

Painting and decorating is a very common service. If you can, make sure your general maintenance staff are capable of undertaking this service or, if not, contract a small but experienced decorator who will give you a good price so that you will be profitable but not overly expensive.

You should be conversant with the following basic points about painting and decorating because these will help you to sell your service when you meet clients:

☐ The differences between oil and water-based paints, between gloss and satinwood, and between matt and silk finishes.

☐ The use of, and importance of, an undercoat.

☐ When two or more coats are required and when they are not.

☐ Drying times.

☐ When primers are required.

☐ Coverage.

Employing a general maintenance operative

Subcontractors are a good stopgap but, in time, you should consider employing your own general maintenance staff. If you do, you will be able to offer all manner of services, including small-scale electrical and plumbing work. There is a great demand for city-centre maintenance work, which can be very profitable. So it is strongly recommended that you employ a general maintenance operative. (It is best to avoid using the terms 'handyman' or 'handy person' – 'general maintenance operative' sounds much better.)

The starting salary for a well experienced general maintenance operative could be £14,000 or £15,000 per annum. You should get plenty of applicants and, if the person you ultimately employ proves themselves to be an asset to your company, you could increase their salary accordingly, particularly if they can offer skilled trade services.

When you advertise for a general maintenance operative, include the term 'handyperson' because this will attract a great many applicants. Some of these applicants will be unsuitable, but you will have plenty of others to choose from. A good general maintenance operative will usually:

☐ be between 35 and 55 years of age, be physically fit and healthy and be male;

☐ have experience of various maintenance roles; and

☐ have one core skill (e.g. plumbing).

They should also be presentable and reliable and have a verifiable work history. To help you decide between strong candidates, you could send them on a trial job. Perhaps a toilet handle is broken in one of your cleaning accounts. Instead of sending the plumber you normally contract, you could send a candidate to see how they cope.

Once you have employed your general maintenance operative, you should provide them with the following:

□ A uniform.

□ A vehicle.

□ A large variety of hand tools.

□ A smaller variety of power tools, such as a drill, jigsaw, etc.

□ Job sheets to complete.

When you send your general maintenance operative out on a variety of jobs, you will need to record the following information:

□ Where they have been, how long they were there and what they did when they were there.

□ What materials they used while they were there.

□ What work is still to be completed.

This can all be recorded on a job sheet, which the client should sign when the work has been carried out to their satisfaction. You could also include a small-works risk assessment on this sheet for health and safety purposes (Figure 14 is an example job sheet you could adapt for your own use).

Quoted works

Quoted works are a regular feature of property services, and it is through quoted works that you will make real profits. Generally speaking, quoted works fall into one of the following categories:

□ **A general maintenance job has become so large that payment on an hourly basis is no longer suitable**. For example, you have been asked to change some light bulbs for a client but, in so doing, you find that two light fittings are not working and that either parts or the whole of the light fittings need replacing.

□ **A client requests 'a quote' verbally for some work they require**. For example, a client asks you to provide a quote to paint part of their office.

□ **A large job for which a quote would be required in any case**. For example, a client tells you they want their office carpet tiles replaced, the walls painted and a partition wall erected.

It takes experience to learn how to price your quoted works, but a handy tip, if not perhaps ethically correct, is to ask an experienced contractor to price the work for you before you quote the client. For example, a client asks you for a quote to paint one of their offices. You

Client				Job number
Site				
Address				

Small works risk assessment: hazards and assessed risk level

People at risk
- Employees
- Contractors
- General public
- Customers
- 2 person team req'd

Please state reason for 2-person team above

	Hazard	Low	Med	High
1	Hot work or surfaces	Low	Med	High
2	Confined space entry	Low	Med	High
3	Slips/trips/falls (ground level)	Low	Med	High
4	Manual handling	Low	Med	High
5	Electricity and other services	Low	Med	High
6	Tools/machinery/equipment	Low	Med	High
7	Sharp objects (glass, tools, etc.)	Low	Med	High
8	Fire/explosion (welding/gas burning)	Low	Med	High
9	Noise/vibration	Low	Med	High
10	Chemicals/dust/fumes	Low	Med	High
11	Work/falls from height	Low	Med	High
12	Compressed air/generators	Low	Med	High
13	Vehicles/fork-lift trucks	Low	Med	High
14	Restricted movement	Low	Med	High
15	Environment (hot/cold/wet/dry)	Low	Med	High

Description of work carried out

Work outstanding/recommendation/reports

State the control measures to be taken to reduce the risk (tick relevant)
- Work area enclosed by barriers, etc. to protect 3rd parties
- Warning signs displayed
- Gloves, goggles, face masks, helmets and/or harnesses worn
- Other risk assessments also used, i.e. ladders and scaffolding, working at heights, etc.
- Shop staff briefed and aware of works taking place
- Other control measures (please state)

- In hours
- Out of hours
- Weekend

Materials or plant used

Quantity	Description

Date	
Tradesperson's name	
Total job duration	

I accept that the tradesperson has completed the work to my satisfaction

Authorised signatory

Print name	
Position	

Fig. 14. Job sheet

are confident your general maintenance operative can do the job but you are unsure what the price should be. You take a painting contractor to the client's premises and ask them what they would quote. They tell you it should take about 6 hours and that the price should be £240, including the paint. You submit this quote to your client and they accept it.

If you were charging *per hour* for this job, as opposed to submitting a quote, using your normal maintenance rates, your charge would be £25 for the first hour and £15 per hour thereafter. The job in fact takes 7 hours, which means a charge to your client of £115. The paint costs approximately £40. The total charge, therefore, would be £155. But you have *quoted* the client £240 and they have accepted this. The profit on the quote is, therefore, an additional £85.

It is easy to see from this how quoted works will benefit your business and your profits. Remember, however, to deliver these services with the same quality and efficiency as you deliver your cleaning services. If you do, you should be overwhelmed with work.

Expanding your property services

RETAIL MAINTENANCE

Because most high-street shops are branches of national companies, they tend to employ 'national' maintenance companies. These 'national' companies are, in fact, anything but national: while they generally have their own core staff in any one particular region, they often also employ subcontractors to carry out maintenance work.

You could contact one of these national maintenance companies and apply to become an approved contractor. If you can, try to arrange a meeting with their designated contractor manager. If you are successful, you will receive good rates of pay and access to that all-important area – quoted works. A word of warning, however. National maintenance companies are notoriously slow payers, and there are frequent insolvencies because of cash-flow problems. Don't put all your eggs in one basket, therefore, and chase your payments as soon as they are due to avoid problems.

REFURBISHMENT WORK

Refurbishment work is extremely profitable so, if it is at all possible, try to take on such work. Refurbishment work includes:

☐ offices;

☐ commercial toilets;

☐ commercial kitchens;

☐ commercially based houses and flats (i.e. those managed by letting agents, etc.);

☐ laboratories; and

☐ insurance work.

Try to undertake as much of this work as you can directly – in other words, using your own staff. However, you should not attempt anything that should clearly be done by an experienced tradesperson unless you are confident and qualified to do so.

Finally, insurance claims are a huge and lucrative market but are also extremely difficult to get into. There is work to be had, however, so probe and pester to find opportunities.

15

ENGAGING SUBCONTRACTORS

❝ *The most important single central fact about a free market is that no exchange takes place unless both parties benefit* ❞

(Milton Friedman, economist)

Subcontractors can be either a great asset or a complete nightmare. While there is no doubt you will need them and that they will be a valuable source of additional income, you should choose and manage subcontractors very carefully.

Pros and cons of subcontractors

You may feel you would like to offer all your services directly, but this may not be financially feasible. There is, therefore, nothing wrong with subcontracting work out – almost all large building and facilities companies do so. There are, however, advantages and disadvantages in using subcontractors.

The **advantages** of using subcontractors are as follows:

☐ You have greater flexibility when you hire subcontractors.

☐ You can use subcontractors for a single job.

☐ You can focus more on what your core staff are good at.

☐ You can start work at short notice, despite any commitments you may have for other work.

☐ You can dictate exactly the requirements of the job.

☐ You don't need to worry about tax and national insurance liabilities.

☐ You can use subcontractors both short term and long term.

The **disadvantages** of using subcontractors are as follows:

☐ You will pay more for a subcontractor to undertake the work than if your own direct staff undertook it.

☐ You and your staff will not gain new skills.

☐ Your direct staff may be unhappy that they are not being given the opportunity to develop their skills further.

□ You cannot control subcontractors directly.

□ Subcontractors may not carry out the work to the same professional standards as you do.

□ Subcontractors may try to poach your clients or may speak badly of you to your clients.

From the outset, try not to let the disadvantages of employing subcontractors affect your business negatively.

Finding and choosing subcontractors

You will find subcontractors through *Yellow Pages*, through the Internet, in business directories, through the direct receipt of their advertising and by word of mouth. When choosing a subcontractor, you should look for:

□ a small company;

□ flexibility;

□ good prices;

□ some kind of credit period;

□ quality workmanship;

□ trust; and

□ professionalism.

It is important to choose the correct size of company. If you employ a one-man band, they may ask to be paid in cash on the day the job is complete, may not be very professional and may let you down because they are spreading themselves thinly between a number of different jobs. A large company, on the other hand, may be more expensive and may expect you to work to their schedule as opposed to your own. They may also supply workers who do not care about, or understand, you or your client's needs. The ideal company, therefore, should comprise more than just the owner but should not be too big. A company comprising two or three staff should be able to cope with the work in a professional manner as well as give you good prices.

You should meet potential subcontractors and outline clearly what you require. Your instinct should help you to decide who is the best, but if you want to find out more there are a number of methods you could use:

□ Ask if the subcontractor is a member of a trade or professional association or is a licensed labour provider with the Gangmasters' Licensing Authority.

□ Find out if they comply with any quality standards, such as British Standards or the International Organization for Standardization standards for management systems.

☐ Obtain personal recommendations.

☐ Ask for references and/or ask to see examples of their previous work.

Any subcontractor who is a member of a trade association will have had to have demonstrated that they have quality systems and training in place, comply fully with health and safety regulations, undertake environmental management and have financial stability, etc.

For a small job, asking for three references would perhaps be unreasonable, and most subcontractors would not be prepared to waste their time supplying these for such little financial return. For large jobs, on the other hand, if the subcontractor is new to you, try to obtain at least two (preferably three) references and follow up on these.

The following are some tips on obtaining references:

☐ Let the subcontractor know you are following up on the references.

☐ Contact the referees in good time so as not to delay the work.

☐ Ask specific questions about the information the subcontractor has provided.

☐ Inquire about the subcontractor's personal qualities, safety record and work standards, and about any legal cases the contractor is, or has been, involved in.

☐ Check the authenticity of telephone references and take notes during the call.

When you receive a subcontractor's quote, read this carefully. You can sometimes be caught out by subsequent 'I didn't allow for that in my quote' comments and thus end up paying more than you expected. The areas that may be subject to change in a quote include materials prices, overtime and night rates. Pay close attention to these and go through them with the subcontractor step by step so that there are no hidden surprises.

Arrangements and agreements

Unless you have obtained an extremely good price from a subcontractor, try not to commit yourself to paying them during the course of the work or immediately afterwards – remember, you will probably have to wait 30 days to be paid yourself. It is the smaller subcontractors who will be looking for a quick payment. Use this to drive their price down: everything is negotiable and, if you are willing to give a little, then so should the subcontractor.

If you use subcontractors on a regular basis, set up a database of subcontractors you know and trust. You could also create a standard written agreement to cover all eventualities:

☐ The subcontractor's responsibilities.

☐ The objectives, scope of the work and the key expectations of their role.

☐ The resources you must provide if the subcontractor needs access to your equipment and/or staff.

☐ The fees and a payment schedule. You may wish to consider penalty or incentive schemes for under- or over-performance.

☐ A procedure for resolving disputes (e.g. review or termination).

☐ Any confidentiality agreements.

Before paying a subcontractor, make sure you and your client are happy with the work. If not, insist that all the faults are rectified and defer making the payment. If you pay before the problems have been resolved, the subcontractor may feel no great urgency to rectify these faults now they have been paid.

Complying with health and safety requirements

There are health and safety requirements to consider when employing subcontractors. For example, you should:

☐ identify the requirements of the job and assess the risks involved;

☐ consult the staff on relevant health and safety issues;

☐ decide what information and training are required;

☐ ascertain a subcontractor's health and safety policies and procedures;

☐ find out about the subcontractor's competence; and

☐ review the way the work was carried out and the risk assessment.

Communication is the key to a smooth-running, safe, working environment:

☐ Provide all the parties with information, instruction and training on anything that may affect health and safety.

☐ Make the subcontractor aware of your health and safety procedures and policies.

☐ Provide management and supervision to ensure the subcontractor's safety.

If you fail in any of the following points, you could find there are not only financial repercussions but also legal ones:

☐ Make sure the subcontractor is competent to undertake the work.

☐ Supervise the subcontractor.

☐ Take steps to prevent contact with live equipment.

☐ Provide information about the existence of asbestos.

☐ Ensure the safe operation of vehicles.

☐ Ensure the safe loading to or unloading from delivery vehicles.

☐ Assess the risks to health from regular exposure to high vibration levels.

☐ Exercise a duty of care towards the subcontractor.

☐ Provide a formal site induction, risk assessment and/or methods statement.

Protecting your clients

When you use subcontractors you will find that, in most instances, you have no choice but to let them communicate with your clients. While this may ease your workload, it could also be dangerous because a relationship may develop between the subcontractor and your client. They might both decide, for example, that there is no need for you to sit in the middle earning money when they could be dealing with each other directly. This is a major quandary when employing subcontractors – being 'back doored' by a subcontractor is difficult to stomach and it could ultimately mean you lose a client altogether.

You could issue a contract to protect yourself from such an occurrence, but the best thing to do is to discuss any concerns you may have about this with your subcontractor. You do not have to say you are suspicious of them – simply point out that issuing business cards or agreeing additional work without your involvement are unacceptable. Most subcontractors will understand this and, if they are getting regular work from you, it will not be worth their while to lose all the work you provide for the sake of one client only. Beware, however – there are plenty of sharks out there who are unscrupulous in this respect.

Appendix I
USEFUL CONTACTS

The following is a list of websites that provide information about different aspects of setting up and running a cleaning business, as well as business in general:

Advisory Conciliation and Arbitration Service (www.acas.org.uk).
Asset Finance (www.fla.org.uk).
Better Payment Practice Group (www.payontime.co.uk).
Bookkeepers' Organization (www.bookkeepers.org.uk).
British Bankers' Association (www.bba.org.uk).
British Insurance Brokers' Association (www.biba.org.uk).
Building Industry Standards Scheme (www.trustmark.org.uk).
Business Angels Network (www.bestmatch.co.uk).
Business Link (www.businesslink.gov.uk) and My Business Rates (www.mybusinessrates.gov.uk/wales) (Wales) (business rates information).
Bytestart (www.bytestart.co.uk) (small-business tax advice).
Chartered Institute of Environmental Health (www.cieh.org).
Chartered Institute of Taxation (www.tax.org.uk) (tax information).
Chic Cleaning (www.reachandclean.co.uk) (wash-and-reach window-cleaning systems).
Cleaning and Support Services Organization (www.cleaningindustry.org).
Cleaning Forum (www.cleanitup.co.uk).
Cleenol (www.cleenol.co.uk) (cleaning chemicals manufacturer).
Companies House (www.companieshouse.gov.uk).
Criminal Records Bureau (www.crb.gov.uk) (England and Wales), Disclosure Scotland (www.disclosurescotland.co.uk) (Scotland) and AccessNI (www.access.gov.uk) (Northern Ireland) (criminal records checks).
Department of Business, Enterprise and Regulatory Reform (www.berr.gov.uk).
Department of Trade and Industry (www.dti.gov.uk).
Department of Work and Pensions (www.dwp.gov.uk).
Employers' Order Line (www.hmrc.gov.uk/employers/orderline.htm).
Envirowise (www.envirowise.gov.uk) (waste management information).
Equifax (www.equifax.co.uk) (business reports and data company).
Federation of Small Businesses (www.fsb.org.uk).
Financial Services Authority (www.fsa.gov.uk) (financial information).
Gangmasters' Licensing Authority (www.gla.gov.uk).
Health and Safety Executive (www.hse.gov.uk/printing/coshhessentials) (COSHH information).
HM Revenue & Customs (www.hmrc.gov.uk).
Immigration Agency (www.workingintheuk.gov.uk).
Institute of Business Ethics (www.ibe.org.uk).

Institute of Chartered Accountants in England and Wales (www.icaew.co.uk), Institute of Chartered Accountants in Ireland (www.icai.ie) and Institute of Chartered Accountants of Scotland (www.icas.org.uk).

Institute of Customer Service (www.instituteofcustomerservice.com).

Internet Advertising Bureau (www.iabuk.net).

Job Centres (www.jobcentreplus.gov.uk).

Low Pay Commission (www.lowpay.gov.uk).

Minorplanet Systems (www.minorplanet.com) (vehicle tracking).

National Federation of Enterprise Agencies (www.nfea.com).

Nilfisk (www.nilfisk-alto.co.uk) (commercial cleaning-equipment manufacturer).

Numatic (www.numatic.co.uk) (commercial cleaning-equipment manufacturer).

Prochem (www.prochem.co.uk) (carpet and upholstery cleaning).

Robert Scott (www.robert-scott.co.uk) (cleaning products supplier).

SEBO (www.sebo.co.uk) (commercial vacuum-cleaner supplier).

Small Business Success (www.smallbusinesssuccess.biz).

Trading Standards Institute (www.tradingstandards.gov.uk).

Tribunals Service (www.employmenttribunals.gov.uk).

UK Domain Name Registry (www.nameroute.co.uk).

Appendix II

THE CLEANING OPERATORS' PROFICIENCY CERTIFICATE

The tasks covered by this course are as follows:

AA1 Chemical competence
AA2 Machines: safe use and care
AA3 Storage of equipment
A1 Mop sweeping
A2 Single-solution mopping
A3 Two-solution mopping
A4 Buffing
A5 Spray cleaning
A6 Machine scrubbing and drying
A7 Strip, dry and reapply emulsion polish
A8A Prepare and reapply a semi-permanent seal using an abrasive mesh disk
A8C Prepare and reapply a semi-permanent seal using a chemical stripping agent
A9 Bonnet mopping
A10 Vitrification
A11 Scrubber drying with a battery-powered scrubber dryer
A12 Scrubber drying with an electrically powered scrubber dryer
A13 Machine sweeping with a battery-powered sweeper
A14 Machine sweeping with a petrol/propane-powered sweeper
A15 Cleaning of stairs, landings, balustrades and handrails
A16 Drum sanding

B1 Suction cleaning
B2 Hot water extraction
B3 Dry-foam shampooing
B4A Wet shampooing
B4B Dry-powder/granules carpet cleaning
B5 Carpet skimming

C1 High-level cleaning
C2 Wall washing
C3 Window cleaning
C4 Pressure washing
C5 Graffiti removal
C6 Dry-steam cleaning

C7   Ventilation extract-grille cleaning

D1   Dust, damp wipe, wash, polish application
D2   Upholstery shampooing
D3   Cleaning toilets/sluices/urinals
D4   Cleaning basins/baths/showers/bidets

E1   Stain removal
E2   Simple access equipment
E3   Cleaning personal computers
E4   Cleaning lifts
E5   Cleaning telephones

F1   Litter picking
F2   Wastes clearance
F2A   Unblocking of waste chutes
F3   Cleaning bin areas
F4   Control of body-fluid contamination and sharps

EQUAL OPPORTUNITIES POLICY

It is the policy of The Cleaning Company not to discriminate against employees on the grounds of sex, colour, race and creed or ethnic or national origin. Employees are reminded that it is a breach of the Race Relations Act or the Sex Discrimination Act on the grounds mentioned above and that disciplinary action may result from any act of discrimination.

In compliance with the Disability Discrimination Act of 1995 it is the company's policy to employ the registered disabled when their disability does not preclude them from carrying out the tasks required and when the working environment is not likely to be hazardous to them on account of their specific disability.

The aim of The Cleaning Company is to comply as an equal opportunities employer through ensuring that no applicant or employee receives less favourable treatment on the grounds of gender, race, disability, colour, nationality, ethnic or national origin, marital status, sexuality, responsibility for dependants, religion, trade union activity and age (up to 65).

Selection criteria and procedures are kept under review to ensure that individuals are selected, promoted and treated on the basis of their relevant merits and abilities. All employees will be given equality of opportunity within the company's service and will be encouraged to progress within The Cleaning Company. To ensure that direct or indirect discrimination is not occurring, recruitment and other employment decisions will be regularly monitored in conjunction with the ethnic records of job applicants and existing employees.

The Cleaning Company is committed to a programme of action to make this policy fully effective.

Attracting applicants

The Cleaning Company will not recruit by 'word of mouth' and will ensure that the wording of all job advertisements does not place unfair restrictions on applicants from different racial groups. The Cleaning Company will not request any additional qualifications that have no bearing on a person's effective performance to carry out the job being advertised.

All adverts placed will state that The Cleaning Company is an 'equal opportunities employer' and that it encourages applications from under-represented groups within the community. The effectiveness of this policy will be monitored by keeping records of the ethnic origins of all staff and applicants.

Selection

The selection of applicants will be based purely on their ability and suitability to meet the requirements of the job and the requirements of each job vacancy that arises will be individually assessed. From this, the right qualifications and experience that the applicant will need to possess can be determined.

Selection tests may be used, if necessary, in as much that they only relate to the specific requirements of the vacant position and that they do not discriminate on the grounds of a person's colour, race, creed, etc.

Promotion

The promotion of an employee within The Cleaning Company will be carried out by the same process it adopts for an application for new employment. Assessments will be based on ability and again will ensure that persons are encouraged to apply from under-represented groups at that level. The Cleaning Company will monitor the ethnic origins of persons selected for promotion and will review and revise promotion procedures as and when necessary to ensure no discrimination occurs.

Training

The Cleaning Company will ensure everyone is made aware that any form of racial discrimination is a breach of the Race Relations Act and is a serious offence which will invoke the company's disciplinary procedure; this will be transmitted through formal training and induction courses.

All persons responsible for the recruitment, selection, promotion and transfer of staff will receive additional ongoing training on how to carry out the requirements of the company's equal opportunities policy and will fully understand both The Cleaning Company's and their own obligations under the Race Relations Act.

Dismissal, redundancy and other detriment

The Cleaning Company will ensure that its policy will not unlawfully or unfairly discriminate on racial grounds in dismissal, redundancy or other detriment to an employee and not discriminate on the basis of gender, race, disability, colour, ethnic and national origin, nationality, sexuality, marital status, responsibility for dependants, religion, trade union activity or age (up to 65).

Members of the above groups will not have disciplinary action taken against them on the basis of performance or behaviour overlooked or condoned when committed by others.

INDEX

accidents, 96
accountant, 132
advertising, 16, 110, 116
agreement, 5, 166
Alliance & Leicester, 36
annual leave, 99
applicant, 63, 64
application, 89
application pack, 19
attitude, 87
audits, 83

BACS, 124
bank, 123
bankruptcy, 144
bedroom, 18
BIC, 4, 64, 65, 81
bin liners, 28
blacksmith, 158
blogs, 41
bookkeeping, 130
brand, 40, 42, 43
branding, 41
brochure, 42
buffing, 128
builders cleans, 13, 50
building work, 158
business cards, 41
business expenses, 140
business guides, 37
business link, 37
business plans, 121

cancellation, 83
capital allowances, 139
carpet cleaning, 23, 24, 52
cash projection, 19

cautions, 135
centre pull, 28
Chamber of Commerce, 37
CHAPS, 124
chemicals, 24
chemical cleaners, 29
CINTO, 2
City and Guilds, 4
cleaning accounts, 54
cleaning materials, 78
cleaning process, 26
cleaning schedule, 70, 74
cleaning solutions, 25
cleaning staff, 11, 15
clearance, 19
clients, 46, 47, 48, 70, 168
client satisfaction, 48
cloths and dusters, 29
colour coding, 107
Companies House, 36
company vehicles, 148
competitors, 30
complaints, 18, 47, 48, 49, 52, 53
compliment slips, 41
conduct, 88
consistency, 20
construction industry, 15
consumables, 28, 53, 71
contacts, 169
corporation tax, 35, 138
COSHH, 106, 150
credit ,141
credit cards, 125
credit terms, 30
criticism, 20

daily cleaning, 10

debt, 141, 143
deep cleans, 14, 18
detail lists, 84
development, 121
disciplinary, 101
discrimination, 100
domestic cleaning, 15, 16, 51

electrical, 156
email, 41
emailing, 113
employees, 59, 69
employee rights, 99
employing, 57, 149, 159
employment law, 98
equal opportunities, 100
equipment, 24
ethics, 88
exit strategy, 122
expanding, 162
expansion, 146

factoring, 145
family, 32
fax machine, 38
feedback, 48
final cleans, 13
finances, 121
financial balance, 20
finding staff, 58
finishing clean, 14
first aid, 68
flooring, 156
follow up, 80, 87
forecasting, 121
forms, 138
franchise, 5
funding, 121

growth, 146

hand over cleans, 13

hand towel, 28
hard floor cleaning, 24
hazards, 68
health and safety, 23, 67, 95, 167
Health and Safety Executive, 67
HM Revenue & Customs, 15
home, 64
home owners, 15
hourly rate, 63
house cleans, 19
housing association, 15, 19, 20

incoming calls, 44
income tax, 139
industrial cleans, 52
initial cost, 36
injury, 68
insurance, 70, 77, 133
insurance cover, 19
internet, 38, 61, 116
interview, 61, 62, 63
invoice, 142
ISO, 19, 27
IT cleaning, 24, 26, 27
IT cleans, 53

Job Centre, 59, 60

laws, 95
leaflet drop, 16
legal, 67
legal entity, 34, 35
leisure cleans, 50
leisure premises, 11
letterheads, 41
letting agency, 15, 18
liabilities, 35
liability insurance, 134
limited company, 35
LLP, 35, 36
local advertising, 60
logo, 40, 41

machinery, 125
maintenance, 155
managed accounts, 19
management staff, 3
managers, 146
margin, 30
marketing, 110
materials, 129
meeting, 70, 74
Merry Maid, 15
minimum wage, 105
mobile phones, 148
Molly Maid, 15
mop buckets, 29
mop heads, 29
motivating, 57
MRSA, 25

naming, 33
national insurance, 136, 137
networking, 42, 118
new-build commercial premises, 14
new-build homes, 14
newspaper, 61
no shows, 91
NVQ, 4

office, 64
office cleaning, 10, 49
office moves, 14
online banking, 124
opportunities, 119
outgoing calls, 44
out of hours, 11
overheads, 49, 125

painting, 158
partitions, 156
partnership, 35
payroll, 137, 150
planning, 95
plumbing, 156

policies, 74, 77
PPE, 14, 69
pricing matrix, 18
printer, 38
proactive, 47, 92
property services, 154
pub cleans, 50
public meeting, 63
pubs, 11

quality, 81
Quickbooks, 132
quote, 48, 72, 74
quoted works, 160

raising capital, 122
reach and wash, 23
reactive, 92
recruitment, 99
refurbishment, 14, 158, 162
refuse sacks, 28
regulations, 95
repairs, 158
repeat clean, 15
responsibility, 67
responsive, 48
retention, 152
rewarding, 57
RIDDOR, 108
risk, 68, 107
risk assessment, 23, 67, 77
running cost, 16

safety, 69
Sage, 132
sales, 120
satisfaction, 20
scrubbers, 127
search engine, 118
self employed, 31
selling techniques, 24
server room cleaning, 27

service, 82
service agreement, 77
shopfitters, 14
sickness, 101
skills, 32, 33
slogan, 41
sole trader, 22, 34
sparkle clean, 14
specialist cleans, 27, 53
spreadsheets, 131
staff problems, 90
staff quality, 20
staff turnover, 20, 66
stain removal, 23
start up, 31
statements, 143
stationery, 41, 115
storage space, 38
subcontractors, 15, 22, 23, 164, 165
success, 39
supervisor, 15
suppliers, 37
suspended ceilings, 156

tabard, 45
tax, 136

tax return, 35
technical rooms, 27
telephone, 43
toilet rolls, 28
trading room cleans, 27
training, 64
TUPE, 102, 104

uniforms, 41, 45
upholstery cleaning, 23, 24

vacuum cleaning, 26
vacuums, 125, 126
VAT, 136
vehicles, 41
versatility, 20

website, 41, 117
welcome pack, 75
winding up, 144
window cleaner, 22
window cleaning, 21, 23, 51
word of mouth, 16

Yellow Pages, 16

1908188R0011

Printed in Great Britain
by Amazon.co.uk, Ltd.,
Marston Gate.